For Christ & Country

For Christ & Country

Understanding the foundation of a Nation

JOHN THOMAS NALL

LitPrime Solutions
21250 Hawthorne Blvd
Suite 500, Torrance, CA 90503
www.litprime.com
Phone: 1 (209) 788-3500

© 2021 John Thomas Nall. All rights reserved.

No part of this book may be reproduced, stored in a retrieval system, or transmitted by any means without the written permission of the author.

Published by LitPrime Solutions   03/25/2021

ISBN: 978-1-954886-04-9(sc)
ISBN: 978-1-954886-05-6(e)

Library of Congress Control Number: 2021902553

Any people depicted in stock imagery provided by iStock are models, and such images are being used for illustrative purposes only.

Certain stock imagery © iStock.

Because of the dynamic nature of the Internet, any web addresses or links contained in this book may have changed since publication and may no longer be valid. The views expressed in this work are solely those of the author and do not necessarily reflect the views of the publisher, and the publisher hereby disclaims any responsibility for them.

Contents

Introduction ix
Dedication xi

A Declaration Of Southern Independence 1
Confederate States of America Lawful Government of the South 4
Our National Birthright 6
(Children in the Darkness) 8
Who Are We? 11
The Republic Of Dixie 19
Passing The Buck 28
Oh Tis The Sweet Land Of Liberty 30
Neo-americans 34
The Confederate Spirit 38
All Hail Caesar! 41
Whos Lost Cause? 45
A Confedcrate Views: 47
More Confederate Views: 48
Confederate Views 49
Confederate Citizens' Peaceful Protest 59
In Recognition Of The Confederate States Of America 61
Patriotism 63
Our Country's Flag 64
Strangers In Our Own Land 66
God's Own Country 68
First Of November Of 2001   (Phasing Out) 77
"The Illusion of the Union" 82
The Constitution 85
Our Nation's Heritage 88
The Offence Of That Symbol 95
Psalms 2: 1-10 97
"To Have Eyes and Yet To Be Blind" 100

Man's Evolution In Error	102
The Moral Conduct of Honor	103
From Nothing Into Something	104
Upside Down Cake	106
The First Layer	111
Our Country's Banners	113
Taxation Without Representation	119
Whose Foreign Policy Is It Anyway?	121
Race Relations In Dixie	124
Slavery	127
(Holy Bible)	130
The Western States	131
Preserving Their Resources	133
Black Powder	135
Lock And Load	138
The N.C. Creed's Objectives	140
North Carolina Creed	141
The North American Profiles	142
The United States Of Mexico	145
Lost In Space	148
Other Truths	150
Understanding Freedom	151
League Loves South	152
The World Trade Center Prayer	153
A Letter Of Recommendations	154
A Day Of Fasting And Prayer	158
Despised by the World	159
"Government Control"	160
Southern Chivalry	161
Knights Of The Golden Circle	162
A Salute To Our Southern Cross	163
We, The People	164
"The Battle Cry"	165
Babylon The Great	166
To Remember Me By	167
Deo Vindice	168
A Southern Toast	169
Statements Of Truth	170
Have You Ever Longed For	177
Confederate National Crest	180
Continuous Balance	181

The Glory Of Jehova	182
In All Glory And Honor	183
In Your Presence	184
Thanksgiving	185
My Hero!	186
"Oh Lord"	187
Soldiers of His Majesty	188
True Love	189
Bendito Sea Jehovah Para Siempre	190
Hear Our Voice	191
Are You Ready?	192
Trinity Of God	193
My Love	194
Lonesome Dove	195
Twinkle Stars Afar	196
In Honoring My Parents	197
My Closing Statement	198

Introduction

As you will soon come to learn, this is not a history book that gives you all of the facts. When it comes to my mind of thought, I have two goals in mind. When I started to write this book, the first goal was to write a book for someone who is a Christian and who is also a patriot. My second goal was to give you a chance to have an open mind, so that you will have a desire to question the things that you were taught in your public schools; but it is your responsibility to study your Southern History and to study the politics of American History, in order to see if you should come to the conclusion as I have. The first step in learning starts with a question. Then it ends with the desire, on your part, to search for the answers. Begin with the question of "I wonder".

God save the South!

At one time or another, John T. Nall was or is a member of:

1. The Southern National Party
2. The Confederate Society of America
3. The League of The South
4. The first chapter Vice President and later to become the second chapter President of The Zebulon B. Vance Chapter of The League of The South, in Rowan County of Salisbury, NC
5. The National Rifle Association
6. The Christian Coalition

Dedication

As a Christian forever and always, and a Confederate from my natural birth to my death, I dedicate this book to my Heavenly Father and His Precious Son, Jesus Christ, Who is my Messiah and King. Even though my spelling and my English grammar, not to mention my handwriting, are poor, it has been from my Lord God, Who has put the words within my heart; and I thank Him with all that I am. I also want to thank my family for their support; and I also want to thank a good friend of mine: Marie Howell of Marie's Print Shop, Inc., in Salisbury, North Carolina, for proofreading all of my material. And I hope that this book will bring joy to my Southern people in the years to come, for Christ and Country!

A Declaration Of Southern Independence

When in the course of human events it becomes necessary for men, in order to preserve their lives, liberties, and properties, and to secure to themselves, and to their posterity, that peace, liberty, and safety, to which by the laws and of nature's God they are entitled. To throw off and renounce all allegiance to a government, which under the insidious pretences of securing those inestimable blessings to them, has wholly deprived them of any security of either life, liberty, property, peace, or safety; a decent respect to the opinions of mankind, requires that they should declare, the injuries and oppression, the arbitrary and dangerous proceedings, which impel them to transfer their allegiance from such their oppressors, to those who have offered to become their protectors.

We hold these truths to be self evident, that all men are created equal; that they are endowed by their Creator with certain rights, that among those, are life, liberty, peace, order, good government, and the pursuit of happiness; that to secure those rights, governments are instituted; that whenever any form of government becomes destructive to those ends, it is the right of the people to alter or abolish it, or to renounce all allegiance to it, and to put themselves under such other government, as to them shall appear best calculated and most likely to effect their safety and happiness; it is not prudent indeed to change for light and transient causes, and experience hath ever shewn, that men are disposed to suffer much before they can bring themselves to make a change of government; but when a long train of the most licentious and despotic abuses, pursuing invariably the same objects, evinces a design to reduce them under anarchy, and the excesses of democracy and finally to force them to submit to absolute despotism, it is their right, it becomes duty, to disclaim and renounce all allegiance to such government, and to provide new guards for their future security.

Such have been out patient sufferings, and such is now the necessity which constrains us to declare and reaffirm our right to renounce all allegiance to Congress, or the Federal government established by their direction.

The history of Congress and its Federal Government since its control by Northern interests in 1860 is a history of continued inconsistency, violation of the most sacred obligations of all public faith and honour, and or usurpation, all having in direct object the producing of anarchy, civil feuds, and violent injustice, which have rendered us miserable, and has established a tyranny of centralized and consolidated federalism over us and our formerly sovereign states.

To prove this, let facts be submitted to the candid world.

While professing a strong belief in the right of self-determination for other peoples and nationalities, they refused this right to Southrons in 1861 with the peaceful formation of our Confederacy, and subjected the South to a brutal war of conquest and a forced reunion at the point of a bayonet, followed by military occupation and a century of exploitation and poverty.

They have subsequently recommended and caused laws to be passed, the most destructive of the public good, and ruinous to individuals.

They have excited and directed our people to alter or annual our ancient constitutions, under which we and our ancestors had been happy for many generations, for the sole purpose of promoting their measures.

They have by mobs and riots and threat thereof awed representative houses repeatedly into a compliance with their resolutions, though destructive of the peace, liberty, and safety of the people. They have consistently through their nonfeasance and misfeasance failed to provide public order and security in the face of an every increasing criminality.

They have, by their misconduct, reduced us to all the dangers and distress of the horrors of civil disorders and riots.

They have erected a multitude of new offices and have filled them with men from their own body, or with their creatures or dependents, to eat out the substance of the people; they have made their officers dependent on their will for the tenure of their offices and payment of their salaries.

They have destroyed all good order and government, by plunging us into the excesses of democracy and the ravages of civil disorders.

They have involved us in an immense debt, foreign as well as internal, and have permitted a massive influx of foreign ownership and control of our local industries, while promoting the export of jobs to foreign lands.

They have involved us in foreign military adventures ostensibly for eleemosynary works and for suppression of criminal intrigues, while failing to provide adequately in either of these areas domestically.

They have engendered among our general population their mendacious beliefs in a perverse secularism characterized by an overweening and ostentatious materialism and hedonism.

They have denied us the right to exercise our Christian heritage in our public facilities and have introduced pernicious doctrines destructive of our Southern heritage into our public schools.

They have fostered and attempted to banish all outward and visible signs of our Southern heritage and nation.

They have imposed an odious and blatant form of gerrymandering, repugnant to all standard of democracy and good government.

They have passed laws favoring minority interest while disfranchising and discriminating against the majority.

They have engendered a foreign economic system which has forced us to forsake our agrarian economy for a rampant and uncontrolled industrialization and urbanization with its concomitant malignancy of environmental damage and blighted cities. Our lands have become the repository for noxious and toxic effluents from Northern regions.

They have wantonly violated our public faith and honour and destroyed all ground for public confidence, or the security of private property, and have not blushed to act in direct contradiction of their most solemn declarations and professions of freedom and equality.

In every stage of these proceedings, they have not been wanting to throw out before us specious excuses for their conduct, as being the result of compromise and supposedly tending to the public good. In every stage since their public conduct began to contradict their public declarations, our minds have been overwhelmed with apprehensions; and as our sufferings have increased, our tears have flowed in secret. It has been dangerous and even criminal for us to display publicly emblems of our Southern heritage or to lament our situation in public.

The unsuspecting confidence which we with our fellow citizens have reposed in Congress and the Federal Government has inspired their successors with very different ideas and emboldened them by degrees to pursue measures directly the reverse of those before adopted as the only just, constitutional, and beneficent towards order and good government.

Through all of these acts they have continually and unremittingly encroached upon the sovereign rights of our States, and we have been reduced to a state of subjugation wherein we are no longer masters in our own house.

We could fill volumes, were we to recite at large their usurpations and violations of their most sacred duties and obligations. We content ourselves with the above brief recital of facts known to the world and attested by their own records.

We have sufficiently shewn that a government thus marked and distinguished from every other, either despotic or democratic, is unfit to rule a free people.

We, the citizens of the south, appealing to the impartial world to judge the justice of our cause, but above all the supreme Judge of the world, for the rectitude and vindication of our intentions, do publicly state and reaffirm our right to renounce and disclaim all allegiance, duty, or submission to congress, or to any government under it, and declare our intention to dedicate ourselves to our right to exercise the right of every people to self-determination and the consequent peaceful establishment by referendum of a new Southern Confederacy, and in support of this declaration, with a firm reliance on the protection of Divine Providence, we mutually pledge to each other our lives, our fortunes, and our sacred honour.

God Save The South.

DEO VINDICE
By John P. George, Jr. Crawfordville, Georgia

Adopted freely from a Loyalist Declaration of Independence, 1781, published in the Winter/Spring 1993 edition of THE POPULIST ALERT, 5575 Chamblee Dunwoody Road, Suite 227, Atlanta, Georgia 30338

Confederate States of America Lawful Government of the South

By Randall Hamilton

We must all remember the truthful events of history and use those truths for the inspiring hope we all share, as an example for today and for all those tomorrows yet to come. Truth is the most powerful weapon ever placed in the hands of man. As Confederates we have this weapon on our side. All truth is of the Almighty God, for He is truth, and we should hold fast to the truth. Our country, the Confederate States of America, was lawfully and constitutionally formed. The lawful citizens of the thirteen member States and Territories known as the Confederate States of America, acting upon their inalienable rights given of Almighty God in creation, via the ballot box, by the consent of the governed, gave birth to a new nation. This was done, not in some dark corner, but by and through their duly elected representatives, at Secession Conventions, or by the direct vote of the citizenry, as was the case in States such as Virginia and Texas. Many States reserved the right to withdraw from the Voluntary Union of States when they ratified the United States Constitution. The United States Federal Government was certainly agreeable to the principle of individual Sovereign States ratifying the constitution, as well as any amendment thereto, since it was drafted into the original document by the Founding Fathers, many of whom later served in that same government and supported the principle. The right of a State to secede was not only set forth as a principle in drafting the original United States Constitution, but was enumerated in the 10th amendment. When the South seceded and formed the Confederacy, they made the Confederate States Constitution the Law of the Southland. The Confederate States General Government, under the Confederate States Constitution, is therefore, unto this day, STILL the only lawful general governing document of these thirteen member States and Territories of the Confederacy. Our occupation government as well as the several State Governments, acting as their cohorts, as the "defacto" governments, because they were instituted by, and a direct result of force. The Confederate States Government and the individual state Governments, elected under the principles of a free sovereign ballot box, and by the citizenry of the Confederacy, are the "de jure" governments or rightful and lawful governing bodies. The Confederate States of America, once formed as a lawful and constitutional entity; a separate, distinct and independent nation and people, was never surrendered as a nation. General Robert E. Lee and the other Confederate States Generals surrendered only the armies they themselves commanded, nothing more. President Jefferson Davis and the men who held the offices of the Confederate States Government were the only ones endowed with the power to surrender the Confederate States of America as a nation. They did not do so! The United States Government, claiming the southern States had been brought back into their "Union of States" could only base that claim on the aggressive use of force. Such acts are committed under force, the threat of force or duress, were not, are not, nor never shall be legal, constitutional and binding. Therefore the Confederate States of America, remains in the status of a conquered, occupied, subjugated and now culturally cleansed nation and people. The acts whereby the various State Governments rescinded their articles of secession, and rejoined the United States, stands as null and void, having been carried out by force, and outside of voluntary and continued consent, as well as outside the Confederate States Constitution. Truth and consent do not come by force, nor are military officers endowed with the power to terminate a duly elected government, nor a lawfully constituted nation. There are provision laid down in the Confederate States Constitution whereby that document may be rescinded, and none of those provisions were adhered to. Therefore, the Confederate States of America is not past tense, but remains as a valid and viable nation upon this earth, awaiting the day of its liberation. When on that day, the now vacant but valid seats in the Confederate States Government shall be filled, via special elections, conducted by the citizenry thereof. On that day, our just and righteous cause shall be vindicated. Let us pray always that we be found worthy of the good graces of the Almighty God. (22 July 1994)

Our National Birthright

It is stated in the 1991 Webster's New World Dictionary that the word *origin* is the meaning of a coming into existence or use; beginning. It is a parentage; birth; lineage. You would also find that in the Webster's New World Dictionary that the word *nation* is a stable, historically developed community of people with a territory, economic life, distinctive culture, and language in common. It is the people of a territory united under a single government; country; state.

Therefore it is clear that our Confederate history has proven that we are a separate and a sovereign Nation known as *The Confederate States of America*. In every way we are qualified as it is written within the Webster's New world Dictionary as a Nation; and we have been since we, the States, left the Union and created and formed our Nation by the grace of our *God Almighty*. It is also clear that the Webster's New World Dictionary also recognized the sovereignty of the State governments, the same States that created the States United of America and the States Confederate of America. The problem with other forms of government is that they do not believe in the sovereignty and rights of other Nations; and they are also determined to create the world in their image and those Nations' governments into their own. These government forms of Democracy, Communism, and Fascism, all fall under this category.

That is why a government of a *Constitutional Republic* is the only true form of government and true freedom and liberty to the citizens of those States. In this form of government the powers are regulated and controlled by the States with guidelines. It also recognizes the sovereignty and the rights of other nations; and it prevents them from interfering with outside problems that are not a direct attack against them. It is sad to say that most of mankind has never learned anything in history and is quick to have selective memory when it comes to political history of the world. Therefore all Empires will continue to enslave other Nations, and they will continue to play the political game of *King of The Hill*.

However, now that we know the truth about our National origin, we must start to proclaim it and work in order to get the United State government to recognize it. Regardless of your race, if you were born in one of the original States of the Confederacy, you are a *Confederate American*; and this will be our first step toward restoring our sovereign independence. We also must condemn all political and military actions of the United State, for as long as they are yoked with their Democracy and continue to hold us under siege; but it should be done peacefully. We must remind them of the Nation that our Founding forefathers intended for them to have. It is in our hope that some day they will restore their

Constitutional Republic and that they (The United States) and we (The Confederate States) shall live beside each other in peace and as neighbors. This is the dream of our Confederate Forefathers. Therefore, we should strive to fulfill that dream and benefit from the fruit of independence that it will bear. Let us pray and let it be in agreement with our Heavenly Father.

(Children in the Darkness)

A crisis has been taking place with our children for some time now, and I am not talking about something that is just taking place in this year. It has been taking place with every generation. Every generation of our children will end up having an identity crisis. This is something that I went through when I was 15 years old. I would listen to Rock-n-Roll with long hair down to my shoulders. I would wear blue jeans and Army boots. In addition, before that, I was picked on by other children because I was a quiet person. Therefore, I learned that a quick punch to the face was a fast way to put someone in his or her place. However, the problem with that was that I was unable to let my guard down because if I did that, people might try to get the best of me. I did not know who I was or the true value of my life. And the thought of us as being some kind of a people had never crossed my mind. In my personal views as a teenager, humanity was evil and would destroy anything that was exposed to it; and the only way to save this world would be to put an end to humankind for once and for all. At the age of twelve years, I became a Christian and took Jesus into my heart; however, I never learned how to bring Him into my world and make my life a part of His.

I can remember as far back as the sixth grade when we were studying history. The subject for one particular day was given the title "the civil war". (As far back as the first grade, I can remember all of us kids pledging Allegiance to the Federalist Flag.) We learned that the southern states, who were in gray, were fighting to keep the black man down and in chains and to destroy the union and its constitution. Moreover, it was we! The United States, who went forward to save the day. A day later, I went to our family's encyclopedia to find a picture of the battle of Gettysburg, Pa. As my dad and I looked at the picture, I asked him which side we were on. His answer shocked me because he said that it was we who were in the gray and not the other way around. I could not understand this because my people did not seem to be evil in my eyes! And we never had that southern flag in our classroom. Time went by, and I did not think much about this issue anymore. Then one day in a ninth grade science class, our teacher started talking about the theory of evolution. That is when I started questioning everything that they were teaching us in school. Being a Christian, and having gone to church most of my life, I said to myself that if they would lie to me about the creation of the universe, then what else would they lie to me about?

That was when I started doing my own research about our history. Questions would come to my mind as to why they thought they knew more about what we fought and stood for, rather than our knowing ourselves. In addition, why did they not have enough evidence to back up their version of the civil war history? I knew that by searching the military history I would come to a dead end. Knowing this, I started to search the political part of history. This was when the answers started to shine light upon our past. After that, I started to study the people themselves. I did some reading on our first president of the

Confederate States of America, Jefferson Davis; and I read about our three-star General Robert Edward Lee". For the very first time, history became a part of my life! Moreover, let us not forget the stories of our beloved General "Stonewall" Jackson. Why, as you would ask me, should this matter at all? I am glad that you ask! In the Bible we read stories about people who are not of our own kind: the Hebrews, the Romans, and so forth; however those Confederate leaders were also men of Character. They were men of Christian Character. Since they were Confederates and of our southern bloodline, I could compare my life to theirs. I wanted to *live* my life, which was much more than this dying world could ever give me. Every day I think of those people of ours during that time; and let us not forget about the ones of which we have never heard in history.

I have come to the understanding that our southern children are being deprived of the natural nourishment of who we are in life and the meaning of life to us as a people, as well as the meaning of being an individual person. Our children should be learning about these things, as stated below.

1. The creationism of life and how it all works in harmony in life.
2. Our Southern Heritage and culture.
3. Learning the foundation of the republic that was brought forth by the founders of the Republic of the United States of America.
4. Learning the evolutionary cycle of improvement upon the Republic, by our forefathers of the Confederate States of America.

Every generation that has been forced into these public schools has ended up with these same problems. These public schools were designed to do more than just teach us basic math and reading. The other goals for these public schools were to transform our way of thinking, our philosophy of life, and how it is intertwined into our society and our personal lives as well, in our laws of justice, and in our philosophy of the powers of the state and federal governments. The goal was to transform us into becoming good Yankee clones, to live like them, to think like them, and to speak like them. This is not the first time such has taken place in history. The United States has been known to have done the same to the American Indians in the past. We are being taught to hate ourselves, to deny the fact that we are a separate people. By doing this, we become less of a problem with which to deal. Not only this, but most of them have a feeling of being superior to anyone else. The only difference I see between the Nazis and the Yankeeites is that when the Nazis feel that you are inferior, they will take your life. However, when the Yankeeite feels that you are inferior, then they will transform you into becoming like them. If you study history, you will learn that Great Britain tried to do this to the Celtic people of Scotland and Ireland. You should also understand that the federal government does not have any constitutional rights to stand on to create and to control public schools.

The responsibility of the schools falls upon the state governments and city governments. Our children need two important things in their lives. The first: they need to know their identity as a people and how this identity became theirs. The second: they need a chance to have a relationship with God. This will give them hope and trust in Him. This will also give them a true understanding of how we fit within the cycle of life. They should also learn how a person can grow and become more than who they were before. They should have examples of how this had an effect upon their ancestors' lives, such as Robert Edward Lee and other men and women during that time. Public schools have always been a failure because they have never been in the hands of the parents. They are more like reconstruction camps for social engineering, places for identity transplants, or federalist camps for children. Another reason that schools should be in the hands of the state and city governments is to have a friendly competition between the states. This would give everyone a desire to strive for a better education system for their children.

Home schooling should be promoted and set up with some sort of standards, such as a golden rule for the children. In addition, laws should be passed that would protect the state governments and prevent their accepting funds from the federal governments to be used in the schools. Every time the federal government gives a loan to or funds to the state governments, they gain more control over the state governments and their city schools. In fact, funding should *never* be given to any state government unless it is a state of emergency! This would reduce the chance for a power play within the system. I would also like to say that home schooling would be perfect for children who are slow learners or who may fall between the cracks of the system. This would make it easier for the teachers to work with those who are unable to keep up with the courses for each grade. Another idea is to have companies, who keep their employees moving from one place to another, pay for the home schooling or part-time teachers for the parents. A bill like this should be given to each state government to be passed. We, the Confederate people of the southern states, should strive to regain control over the education, the security, and the value of the meaning of life for our children. Whatever we allow to take place during one generation of children within this present day shall indeed do more harm or more good to the next generation.

30 August 2001 John T. Nall

Who Are We?

So many times I have heard my people call themselves *Americans*. In addition, I have wondered if anyone truly understands just how false that statement is. The title *The United States of America* or *The Confederate States of America* defines the location of each country. The people in South America are just as much Americans as the people in North America. If you were to say that you were from North America, it would be much closer to the truth than to say that you are an American. However, it still would not define your National Identity. If you visit South America and ask them is they are Americans, most of them will say yes. If you then ask them, *Are you from El Salvador or are you from Mexico?*, the answer would also be yes. If you ask someone from Mexico if they are from *The United States*, their answer would also be yes. This is not to say that they are from *The United States of America*; however, they are from *The United States of Mexico*. By the way, *The United States of Mexico* has 32 states. The people in South America find it a joke when they hear someone from North America proclaim themselves to be Americans. If I was writing a story on the subject of our Southern People or of the Northern People, most of the people within North America would understand who they were reading about. However, for us to say that we are Southerners or that they are Northerners would still not be a true statement, because this only tells the reader about the location of my subject, not the country nor where they are from. I am just as guilty for using those words *Americans* or *Southerners*, although I have heard them for most of my life. I have also heard my own people make statements about the U.S. Flag as being an *American Flag*. It is true that the flag of the United State (and that is without the "s" on the end) is from North America, but it does not tell you the name of the country. I have heard comments about people using the title *American flag* and *Confederate flag* within the same subject.

First things first! The American flag could be any State Flag from any Country from North America to South America. The second problem is that every Flag of the Confederacy is from North America, meaning that they are all *American Flags*. That is to say that they are flags from *The Confederate States OF AMERICA*, even though the federal government of *The United States* has replaced their government of the Republic with the government of Democracy. In addition, the sovereignty of each State is no longer enforced as it once was. That is the meaning of *To control the laws and to protect their borders as they once did*. The title *The United States of America* needs to be changed to *The United State of America*.

Something else you need to understand is that under the Republic, by the federal constitution of that government, which would have been the constitution of the Confederate States of America and of the United States of America, a person would have been a citizen of the state in which he lived. Once the United States did overthrow the Federal government of the Confederate States of America and forced them by conquest, back into the Union, then a slow transformation took place. Once the Republic had been replaced with the more revolutionary thought of Democracy, the people's citizenship changed from being a State citizenship to a Federal citizenship, which is what they like to call an *American citizenship*.

As a state citizen, you are protected not only by the federal constitution, but also by the state constitution of the state in which you live. You have the right to buy property without more taxes being added to it. Once your property has been paid off, you no longer are required to pay taxes on it. It is the state in which you live that is charged to protect your rights and to keep the federal government from stepping out of line. In addition, taxes are not taken out of your paycheck; and when you buy something, you also pay a small tax on the product. Moreover, you only pay that small tax on that product just that one time. The income that is used to support the federal government comes from the imports and exports of trading only.

As Federal citizen, however, you have a right to move from one place to another, but everything belongs to the federal government. You cannot truly own any property, because if you were to stop paying taxes on your property, even after you had paid it off, your property would be taken away from you. The federal government has full control over the amount of liberty they will give you from time to time. Moreover, being a Federal citizen does not hold the same value to the rights that were written in the constitution. You must understand that the state constitution of those state governments shall no longer be a protection to the people of their states. The federal citizens and the citizens' children are, in truth, property of the federal government, as their liberties are being regulated on a day to day basis. So ask yourself this: If your freedom was protected by the constitution of the United States, then why do you need organizations to fight for the very basic freedoms that are already written within that document? And why is it that the debate is always about the definition of what those liberties are?

1. Instead of saying that someone is an U.S. citizen, the correct statement would be that someone is a Federalist citizen.
2. Instead of saying that you are from America, you should say you are from North America or the *United State* (without the letter "s"), or that you are from *the Confederate States*.
3. Instead of saying the *American Flag*, you should say the *Federalist Banner* or the flag of the *United State* or *Confederate States*.
4. Whenever someone is talking about an *American Flag*, it is important that they make it clear as to what country they are talking about.
5. Instead of someone saying that they are a *southerner*, the correct description is that they are a *Confederate*. It would be all right to say that they are *a Confederate American by birth*.

In this book, you will find that whenever I am making statements about my southern people, I always call them *Confederates*. Before we go any further, I will explain why:

Statements of Belief

1. I believe: That the states with withdrew their membership from the union were justified.
2. I believe: That the Confederate states were forced back into the union by actions of war.

3. I believe: That the United States has no Constitutional and legal right to justify this action.
4. I believe: That the Southern people of these states are, in truth, citizens of the states in which they were living.
5. I believe: That the Southern people are not Americans but, in truth, Confederates instead.
6. I believe: That the Confederate States of America is still a separate country without self-rule.
7. I believe: That the Constitution of the Confederate States of America is still a legal document within the Confederacy.
8. I believe: That the National Anthem of the Confederate States of America is still ***GOD SAVE THE SOUTH.***
9. I believe: That the loss of the Confederate States' federal government and its military does not cause that country to stop being a separate country.
10. I believe: That the Federal citizens or U.S. citizens are unconstitutional within the U.S. constitution.
11. I believe: That the Confederate people are Federal citizens by conquest by the present Federal forces that are occupying Confederate soil.

Now I would like to take time to explain my point of view for each one, beginning with the first.

1. The states that withdrew their membership from the union were justified in doing so. The Declaration of Independence represented the voice of the people, which is the voice of the people within those states in which they live. It has nothing to do with the voice of the Federal government. The Declaration of Independence does not only represent the voice of the people within the North American States. It also represents the voice of every person on earth who loves freedom. Just to make it clear: the Federal government does not have a voice. The Federal government only has those powers that were given to it by the Constitution of the United States and of the Confederate States. The Southern states that left the union after South Carolina did so, not because of slavery but because of more union federal troops that were sent into Fort Sumter. The Southern States knew that once Union troops were sent into the state of South Carolina, against the will of that State government, then the sovereignty of South Carolina was violated. Because of this action by the United States government, the southern states understood that every state within the union was in danger of losing their independence and their sovereignty.

2. The Confederate states were forced back into the Union by actions of war. The United States Government had proclaimed that the southern states were in an act of rebellion and were to be treated as such. Yet, after the southern states had been defeated, they were not allowed to take their place within the United States Congress, not until they had rewritten their state's constitution in order to make the southern states loyal to the United States government. A *ratification of submission*, if you will. Once our country had been overthrown by the United States, the southern states had a choice of either being treated as conquered territory or submitting to the ratification of their states' constitutions. They were required to make changes in the States'

constitutions that would be acceptable to the government of the United States. The citizens of each state did have all of their rights taken away from them for fifteen yeas. Before that, the members of the state governments and of the Federal government of the Confederate States of America was put into prison, without trial, never having been proven guilty in a neutral court of law.

3. The United States has no constitutional and legal right to justify its actions. The State Government of South Carolina tried more than once to work out the problems with the United States Government over the issue of Fort Sumter. The United States refused to listen and work out these issues. When more troops were sent into Fort Sumter, the State of South Carolina knew that this was an act of war by the United States government. This action of aggression by the President of the United States (Abraham Lincoln) was without authority to use the military in such a way, to pick a fight. The Constitution of the United States does not give any powers to the president for using the military to start a conflict or as a military police force, nor to use the military as a weapon to force social issues upon the citizens of each state. I am also talking about other Presidents of the United States as well. The constitution of the United States does not give the Federal government any power to deny the rights of any state to secede, nor to interfere with the policies of any of the state governments, who are protected by the U.S. Constitution.

4. The Southern people of these states are, in truth, citizens of the states in which they are living. You must understand that the constitutions of each of the states, as well as the Federal constitutions of both the United States and the Confederate States of America, do not recognize or mention anything at any time about becoming a Federal Citizen. Not once have I seen anything or any statements from our Founding and our Confederate ancestors on this subject. I also must say that the States who are legal members of the union are also citizens within the states in which they live and not *U.S. citizens*. The question about the *State of West Virginia* is another subject. Only once have I found in the U.S. constitution a mention of being a citizen of the United States. Moreover, I have found a similar statement in the Confederate States' constitution about being a citizen of the Confederate States; however, this statement was about being a citizen from a member state of the union and of the Confederacy. The rest of the time, statements have to do with being a citizen from each of the states. I should also point out that being a Federal citizen was something that was created by the actions of Democracy, which had overthrown the true form of government of the United States, that of a Republic.

5. The Southern people are not Americans but, in truth, Confederates instead. The Federal government of the Confederate States of America has never signed a peace treaty or signed papers of surrender to the United States government. The states of the Confederacy were denied the right to vote on the issue of rejoining the Union. The States' governments were denied the right to act on behalf of the voice of the Confederate people from each state. After the invasion by the United States, the Confederate people no longer had a voice. The military leaders do

not have the right to speak on behalf of the surrender of the Confederate States of America. The Confederate States of America had a Federal government, army, navy, monetary system, Confederate States constitution, the Third National Flag, the Great Seal of the Confederacy, peace treaties with the North American Indians, and a National Anthem, *God Save The South*. The Confederate States were on good terms with Great Britain until that propaganda started coming from the United States, which was, by the way, over the issue of slavery. Also, Great Britain was threatened by the United States for helping the Confederate States. If this does not depict a separate country, then I do not know what does! It is clear that our ancestors believed that they were a separate people and a separate country as well. We will talk more about this subject from time to time.

6. The Confederate States of America is still a separate country without self-rule. The Federalist people believe that military power defines what is right and is in force as being law. The Confederate people believe that once something has been written and approved by the people it is therefore the law, until the time comes for it to be changed by the people. The Confederate people view the documents of our Founding Fathers in the same way that they view the Ten Commandments, knowing that the Heavenly Father would never change The Ten Commandments. Thus, in the same way that the liberties were written never to be done away with to further the desires of a Federal government for more power. Once extra Union federal forces were sent into Fort Sumter, the other Southern States realized that the letter of the law, which by the way was the Constitution of the United States, was no longer intact. This has become a dead letter and the government of the Republic, which was guaranteed by that constitution, is now a dead Republic. This was when the other states of the south began to abandon ship. For as long as God had given life to humanity, slavery had been part of the system that has created great and powerful nations, as well as bringing some of them to their knees. Slavery has expanded from civilized societies to savage societies, from every country to the open field and wild territorial areas. When the state of South Carolina withdrew their membership from the union, it was because they could see the writing on the wall. The fall of the great Republic was about to begin. The state of South Carolina did leave the union over the issue of slavery; however, there was much more to the story than just that. There has been a movement within the federal government from that very moment, to replace the Republic form of government with a more centralized form of government. Today it is known as Democracy. This, during the time of our Founding Fathers, was termed The Federalist and the anti-Federalist. The southern states believe that Mr. Abraham Lincoln represented the Federalists, in one form or another. They believed that he could not be trusted. The controversy over slavery affected two other areas that would have destroyed the slave states. Slavery was the only thing they had as a tool for voting. Moreover, to vote is to express your voice. The other area was how this would have affected the economy of each slave state. If it was O.K. to do away with slavery within the constitution, then what might happen to other rights that were supposed to be protected by the constitution. The Northern news supported the idea of the Southern States leaving the Union. To let the southern states leave freely would not only give

the northern states more control over the government, but they also believed that this would be less burden on the union. Not long after this, the news had reached the northern press that the Southern States were going to set up free trade with other countries. They feared this, in that it might destroy the economy of the Northern States. On the side of the Northern States, you had the Federalists, the Abolitionists, and the Industries. In the Southern States, you had the Anti-Federalists, the Secessionists, and the Farmers.

After over 130 years, which is a very short time in history, our people have gone through changes, resulting in something of a split personality. One minute they were Confederates; now they are calling themselves Americans. I can give two reasons for this. The transforming of the thoughts of people has been accomplished through the use of public schools, a method once used on the North American Indians. They were taught that they should be ashamed to be Indians, that they must reject the ways and ideas of their people. Who knows what else? One reason it didn't work too well was because it was not practiced long enough. The same method was used on our Confederate people; and after over a hundred years of this, we can see the destruction that has taken place. The same method is also used on the citizens of the United States. Let me give you some proof. The teaching of evolution, which is nothing more than a theory, is practiced. Sex education and the promotion of having sex with the same sex is promoted. Mythology is taught and called *U.S. History*. I would go so far as to say that the U.S. history books could put Mother Goose's stories to shame. I should also say that at times those federal history books may have quite a few half-truths therein. Let us not forget the brainwashing, started in the early school grades. I am also talking about the forcing of our children to pledge allegiance to that federal banner. I will talk more about that later.

When one country is powerful enough to overthrow another, is force enough to cause that weaker country to become a part of the more powerful country, or empire? Does this mean that the defeated country is no longer a separate country? If you say "NO!", your answer is correct. However, if your answer is "Yes", then the public schools have done a good job in controlling your thinking process. To say yes is to think in the terms of a tyrant. During World War II, after Germany had defeated Poland and France, the people from Poland were still Polish, and the people from France were still French. Empires who have defeated other countries would force these countries to serve, to fight and die for them, as well as to fight and die under their banner. At times, in some empires, the weaker countries were denied their identity as a people, including their National identity apart from the empire that they were serving. Sometimes, when a country has been dominated for so long, they start to cling to that which has denied them liberty and life. The opinion of the United States government, concerning Confederate States being a separate country, is that since the rebels lost the war, this should also mean that the Confederate States could not be a separate country. When this statement is made, it shows that their view is based on conquest and military power, which means that the constitution of the United States and the Declaration of Independence have no voice in this subject. The Yankees believe that conquest always decides what is right and what is wrong.

1. The Constitution of the Confederate States of America is still a legal document within the Confederacy. Before our beloved sister state of South Carolina had ever left the Union, secession was taught at West Point. From the moment West Point was established up until 1860, secession

was taught in their classes. Some of the northern states had made statements about leaving the union from time to time as well. The Confederate States took the old constitution of the United States and made some improvements on it. They did this in order to bring it up to date, just to make sure that it would be harder for its meaning to be twisted. They went back to clarify what was written in this document. The constitution of the Confederate States of America is and always will be the letter of the law here in this occupied Confederacy. Our constitution of the Confederate States was adopted unanimously on 11 March 1861, at Montgomery, Alabama. Because the Confederate States were invaded by the United States and enslaved back into the Union, the Constitution of the United States cannot and is not a legal document within our Confederate borders.

2. The National Anthem of the Confederate States of America is still GOD SAVE THE SOUTH. Our national anthem was entered, according to the Act of Congress, AD 1861, by Miller & Beacham in the Clerk's Office of the District Court of Mid. (Written and composed by Earnest Halphin) A strange fact, and yet the truth, is that during the 1950s, the television show Ripley's Believe It Or Not made a statement that the United States did not have a National Anthem. In addition, if it had not been for that television show, the United States would not have a National Anthem today. This means that the Confederate States' National Anthem is much older than that of the United States.

3. The loss of the Confederate States federal government and its military does not cause that country to stop being a separate country. The New World order is coming! And what shall become of the people of the United States? Will they be ready to take down their United State flag in order to replace it with the flag of the United Nations? Or will it be some other form of one-world banner that the United State federal government will have in mind *in the* near future? You might believe that this could never happen. However, since this has already happened to the Confederate States of America, and since you are trusting the federal government of Democracy to teach your children, anything can happen. One of the biggest lies that they have taught is that it was the Confederacy who was fighting for Independence. In truth, independence had been given to them from our Heavenly Father, the documents of our Founding Fathers, and the people who fought and died on the battlefields. That independence is the very sovereignty that was established for each state, (meaning that it is the constitution for each and every state). The southern states had only acted within the safety and protection of their state independence. The future of our people and our country does not depend on trusting our federal or state governments. It depends upon trusting our Heavenly Father and His Son, as well as the responsibilities that we as a Confederate people have. in embracing and acting out the liberties and truth according to the meaning of each liberty that we have been blessed with, as they were paid for, in full, by the blood of our ancestry.

4. The federal citizens or the U.S. citizens are unconstitutional within the U.S. constitution. The people within the union have been denied the right to proclaim their state citizenship without

the fear of losing the liberties they have left. The United States has done the same thing to the citizens of the Confederacy. Liberty is not something you bargain for. It is not something that you have to ask for or request. The very basic freedom comes with the responsibilities of actions and protection to the people, with our Heavenly Father's blessing. Any form of government does not create nor protect our liberties; however, the people from each state should always protect it. To use the governments as a tool and not as a weapon against the liberties of their own people is the duty of government. A government is good as long as it functions according to the foundation on which it was built. Even a foundation has boundary lines, limiting what that government can enforce upon others.

5. The Confederate people are federal citizens by conquest and by the present federal forces that are occupying Confederate soil. The war against the Confederate people has never come to a close, although the methods have changed in many ways. The United State is riding shotgun over our state governments at all times. They still have military bases within our state borders. They are still using public schools to control what form of information and the amount of information that will be given to our children. They are using the public schools for social engineering in the lives of the children. They are using our people to fight and to die in order to create this Yankee Empire of Democracy. We are being taxed to death and used as cheap labor. Our jobs are always in danger of being moved to Mexico or somewhere else. We are denied the right to be ourselves as Southerners and Confederates. They are forcing multiculturalism upon us. In addition, in due time, they will destroy us as a people, without firing a shot. We are becoming the very things that our Founding Fathers and our Confederate forefathers fought and died to protect us from. Read the Declaration of Independence of the United States. in addition, learn and understand the meaning of those words.

The Republic Of Dixie

A Country which is against itself shall not stand much longer. The conflicts of different views can cause a barrier that would prevent our people from uniting as Southerners of the Confederacy. Our visions for our future are not yet clear to us, because we are still struggling over the issues that have crept into our minds since the aftermath of being occupied. We limit our abilities within our arms' reach. Yet, we long to have the right to stand together as a people once more, a Southern people of different races sharing the same Southern land and Heritage; neighbors to one another as we strive to respect each other's space and differences; fighting and dying beside one another as we struggle to protect our homeland and Country from being invaded. Being denied the right of allowing any present racial strife among us to be healed within a Christian society, a continual wedge is forced upon us that has divided our views into little broken pieces. Twisted experiments in social restructuring of our everyday living is transforming us as a people from Dr. Jekyl to Mr. Hyde. Our people have a vision that has been blurred with half-truths and fantasy. We are seeking for the truth, because it is much purer than gold. Through the doorway of truth is an open invitation to that which we are calling to be a reality.

For where is the justice to all of the descendants and of our ancestors of different races that had worn the honorable Grey? I can tell you that it is not man that is able to restore the honor and the liberty that belongs to us, only the most high who knows and sees all can do this. Let the truth of our history be our Testimony to our Great Maker, for as a people and a Country we are proud of who and what we are, as His Creation. Moreover, we always are to humble ourselves before His Grace and mercy. We are Southerners by birth and Confederates by birthright. Nevertheless we are never too far from falling down in sin and becoming lost without Him. We seek not to destroy nor to conquer those nations around us. We care not to invade any Country and make them yield to our military strength, not even to force our ways upon them. No! We do not believe in destroying the difference of other peoples of other countries. All we are saying is this: As a Nation under the grace and guidance of almighty God, and as a Confederate people who have suffered for generations under the persecutions and discriminations of the Union forces and policies, we desire every other Nation to mind their own affairs and we shall do the same. To do so is the first step in establishing peace between our Countries. A day will come when The Confederate States of America shall be a free Country once more. It will not be done with violence or actions of terrorism; nor will it be done by overthrowing the United States government. Our ancestors have already bled and died for our freedom. Adding more deaths would not change anything. However, we do have four weapons that we can put into use right now. The first thing to do is to plead our cause to our Heavenly Father, asking Him to deliver us as peacefully as possible from the Yankee's occupation.

The second thing that we need to do is to share the Gospel in every state that is within the Union. We would be doing our duty, which may save many souls, and it would be pleasing to our Lord God.

The third thing we must do is to share the history of our people and country within the states of the Union. To have debates and open discussions about anything they may not understand about us would scare away all of those scary stories about us Southern Bible Thumping trailer trash. In addition, let us not forget that dreaded Redneck Phobia. We should strive to have character as a people and as individuals, with the help and guidance of our Heavenly Father.

The fourth thing we need to do is to become self-conscious about the unnatural changes that are flooding and destroying our identity and our southern society as a people. All forms of education and communications that are beyond our control are being used for controlling our people and for propaganda purposes. We, as a people, should have control over our own identity and liberty, without control from outside influences. The Southern bloodline of our people is more precious than all the wealth and materialism on this earth. Our blood is too valuable to spill in the name of the Yankee Empire and their conquests.

When the time comes that we are no longer under the yoke of the Yankee scepter, then we will be able to have the entire socialist and fascist organizations forever removed from our Confederate borders, for they are both using racial supremacy and mongrel society as a catapult in promotion their ideology. Moreover, let us not forget the persistent interference of the United States government. The United States Government has, for too long, been using the people as racial blocks in voting over races. They had established racial strife in the Confederate States long ago by using Yankee Negro troops to punish the white Southern population for withdrawing and leaving the Union. They have limited the amount of power within the Confederacy, so that the racial populations will fight each other over the bread crumbs of power. Racial strife is one way to keep the Southern people divided. This is done in order to deter the desire for Independence. Different forms of racial genocide are also an effective tool to be used. Another form of division among the people is evident in the country of Ireland, for so long as the people continually have a division among themselves over the issue of religion they shall never be able to establish true independence from Great Britain. Where in the Bible does Jesus Christ give His permission to his brothers and sisters in His Name to kill someone else with different religious views? Not once in the New Testament, nor does He give His approval of any such violence and death such as Ireland is committing against herself through self-extermination. Ireland does not deserve Independence until she is able to solve her own problems with the help of God and with no outside interference from Great Britain.

The best weapon that can be used to break the will of a people, without using much force, is to take away and deny them anything that they, as a people, could use; anything that would make them stand together as a people and as a nation. In effect, this amounts to destroying their identity and understanding of their liberties, their history, their race, their customs, their philosophy about life, their language and accents, their religious beliefs, anything that helps the people stand together and be proud of themselves. These things must be broken down and done away with. All symbols and landmarks must be destroyed. All of their history should vanish from within the pages of history and be replaced with something else that would make them more docile. They must have some form of thought of selfcontrol while they are being transformed into something else. Some people believe that the Reconstruction period was about rebuilding the cities of the Confederacy; however, it goes much further than that. Reconstruction 1 was the transformation of our political views and functions of our state governments into this new Democracy.

The second part of the period of Reconstruction 2 is taking place at this very moment. In fact, you have just read it in this paragraph. Multiculturalism will be the final blow in destroying both Nations. The western states of the union have more culture and heritage than all of the rest of the Union states. If the Southern states of the Confederacy should establish a close friendship with any of the other states of the union, then it should be with the Western states, because we have much more in common with each other. Also, we are both looked down upon by the rest of the states of the Union.

Information concerning any persecutions of our Confederate people is intentionally being suppressed and ignored by the news media. Southerners have been murdered for having Confederate flags on their cars or trucks, sometimes for wearing Confederate T-shirts. Our children are being discriminated against in public schools and are being suspended for wearing or having a Confederate flag on them or in their possessions. Our people are being discriminated against in the work force and have been fired for having a Confederate bumper sticker on their toolbox or lunch box. In some places, our people are not allowed to park their automobiles on company property because of their having a Confederate bumper sticker on their cars. Our people are being discriminated against in the communications field because of their southern accent in their language. They are forced to eliminate their accent whenever they are speaking on your local and national news. Whenever our people decide to stand up and to have a peaceful demonstration against such violations of our civil rights. The news media will turn their heads the other way. Other times they will make up excuses of being tied up on another news spot. Any time that our people show any form of Confederate patriotism or pride in our heritage in public, suddenly the news media and press become anti-Confederate and antisouthern. The Northern-controlled carbon copy media and press becomes biased against the Old Confederacy and her people. It is one thing for them to promote pro-issues of the United States and their National banner; however, whenever it has anything to do with the Confederate symbols, it is always played down, as being something that is an evil thing. Destruction of our Confederate cemeteries and statues, including our monuments, goes on without notice. The majority of our people will never hear about it, and the rest of them couldn't care less. The reason that the rest of our people couldn't care less is that they cannot care about something if they do not know and understand anything about it. False delusions of patriotism and materialism as well as those reconstruction camps called public schools, have done a great job in turning our people into mindless zombies that can be controlled by their own emotions, just like puppets on a string. Indeed, reconstruction has done a better job than the determination to exterminate our people by the Union forces during the war.

Southern Negroes will come out and march with us from time to time. They will come out in public places while wearing their Confederate uniforms. Sometimes they might be marching in a heritage march, with a Confederate battle flag wrapped around them like a cape that you might see in a cartoon super hero magazine. I one time saw a Negro couple walking together while waving their battle flags. It was strange, at first, to see them on our side of the battle flag debate. However, it was a blessing to have them with us. Many of them have known for some time of their ancestors who fought and died in the defense of our Country, but the fear of persecution from their own people hangs over their heads like a storm cloud that is ready to strike them down. Racist remarks are made toward their own people. Disparaging comments have been directed toward them such as "You're nothing more than a white man's nigger". This goes to show you how stupid and ignorant some people are. I am sure that there have been other racial comments that have been made toward them by their own people from time to time. They do this in order to keep their own people in line and to keep our Confederate people from coming together. I have also heard that, at times, their lives have been threatened and that some have been beaten by their own race, just for standing up like true Southern compatriots. They are, indeed, true Confederates in every sense of the word. Nevertheless, true stories like these will not find their way into the news realm of the media. These people who have a hatred toward our people and all that we represent are striving to make this sound like some kind of white man's war when, in truth, just bout every Southerner of race who had lived within the Confederate States stood together in defense of our homeland and country. Here in our beloved states of the Confederacy we do not need the guidance, protection, and teaching of the United States government. We just need them and their military might to remove themselves from our state borders.

It is written, within our constitution of the Confederate States, that we the southern people of the Confederacy have given ourselves over to God, that our lives and future shall be in His hands and His hands alone. Now these are not the exact words that are actually written, however, they are close enough to make my point. At times I may say harsh words toward my people; nevertheless, I understand that sometimes all of the facts and truth will not always get their attention. I do, however, have a deep love and concern for our people and our future. In addition, I do not care what foreign flag is flown over our Confederate soil, not even if our conquerors (the United States), were to change us over into the hands of some other Nation. We shall always be a separate country, and a day shall come when those Nations who rule over us by force shall stand before God and give an account of their actions. In peace and war, all countries must give account for all things, even for the secrets, which they may have done in the dark. In western movies and on book covers you will find pictures of a National flag of the United States; nevertheless, you won't find any National flag of the Confederate States. However, you will find the battle flag or Navy Jack of the Confederate States' military. This is done in order to downplay and reject the fact that their were two countries at war with each other. Instead, we have been put in the category of playing the role of civil disobedience or civil strife. The statements like *The Civil War* or *The War Between the States* still serves the same purpose and goal. They also say that it was a war of *Brother against Brother* and other similar statements. The war of *Brother against Brother* is a very natural function in our Celtic heritage. When the colonies were fighting for independence from Great Britain it was brother against brother. Any time that your family has an open discussion over politics and religion you will sometimes find a division of beliefs within your family. In other words, God has given each man, woman, and child, the freedom to think for themselves. Free thinking like this is un-American and unexpected under the regime of the Yankee Empire. However, I would like to cover some of the views that our people come up with since that unnecessary war, in order to correct and clear up the confusion that goes along with it.

It was constitutional for the Southern States to leave the Union. However, now that they have lost the war they are part of the United States. The real question is this: What is supreme over the other? Is it the laws that were written down on paper and paid for in full by the blood of those who fought and died to protect and transfer those ideas of liberty to their families' next generation? On the other hand, shall some form of government have the power to contradict and override anything that has been written down and was paid for by blood? If the last is your choice, then I must ask you this: What logic would it be to write something down that was never meant to be kept in force? In addition, what value is it for someone to believe in something enough to die for it and then have it vanish, in the presence of their family? For is it not that it was more for the ideas that they believe in? Much more so than just for the fact that it was written on a piece of paper. Yet, once those ideas had been established upon that paper with the down payment of life and hope, then those ideas were officially established as a reality for them. This is why the Declaration of Independence and the constitution of the United States of America shall always and forever be their legal documents. Even if the United States were to some day become a conquered country and occupied because of war, those documents would still be legal and constitutional, yet not active because of the presence of foreign forces within the Union.

It is on these same principles and in the same spirit that the Declaration of Independence of the United States stands. In addition, it is from the sovereignties of each constitutional state of the south that the rebirth of the federal constitution came forth, during the process of evolutionary phases. Moreover, by doing so, thus was a new Nation born.

The federal government is supreme ,over all of the state governments! **Not true!** The constitution of the Union or of the United States was designed to work in harmony with each of the states' constitutions. If the federal government is supreme, then there would have been no creations of other states and their governments. The constitution of the United States was not created by powers that were taken away from the states. It was created by the powers that were granted to the federal government from those states that had established the constitution of the Union. Nor is the federal government on a level or equal playing field with the states. The federal government only has the powers that are written within the constitution. Any other powers belong to each of the member states. It is the question of who are the real servants and master.

Secession might be necessary once more for the Southern States. Secession is a natural and a constitutional right by a sovereign government. Remember that the constitution was written to regulate the powers of the federal government, not that of the states. Secession falls under the category of **ALL OTHER POWERS BELONG TO THE STATES**. If secession was legal then, it must still be legal. Being an established fact that those southern states did leave the Union, they must still be no part of the Union. The Southern States rejoined the Union against their will and under the might of the Union military. Moreover, the Southern States are still members of the Confederacy. This can only make the United States' actions invalid and unconstitutional. Therefore these actions should not be recognized as a reality. If secession had not been established by those Southern States, then those states could at any time withdraw their membership in the future. A state that is a member of the Confederacy cannot join the union or any other Nation until that state withdraws its membership from the Confederacy. The same goes for any state that is in the Union. I should also say that it is not necessary to fight for the right of secession or Independence. Once the colonies defeated Great Britain, this led to the constitutions of each state, for it is these documents that establish the sovereignty and independence for each state.

What about those Southern states which were denied the right to withdraw their membership from the Union? Those states were invaded by Union force in order to overthrow their state governments. It still has to be done by the book, just as is done with every bill that is passed by their government, regardless of the fact that the Union troops had taken them to prison and closed down their state governments. These states were denied the right to withdraw their membership from that Union. Therefore they are still members in the Union; however, at any time that they desire to do so, they can withdraw.

It is said that there is a statement within one of the Southern states' constitution that it is not legal for that state to leave the Union. Once the Confederate states' military was defeated, the representatives had gone back to the U.S. Congress to take their seats. During the entire war, it was said that the Southern states had never left the Union, for it was treason to leave the Union. Yet, once the representatives got to the U.S. Congress to take their seats, they were denied that right. They were told by the Congress of the U.S. that their states were no longer members of the Union and that their Southern states had a choice of being treated as conquered territories or taking their seats, provided that they submit and make changes that would be pleasing to the U.S. Congress. No one wants their State to be treated like some kind of conquered territory. So part of the changes to their states' constitutions, by the guidance of the U.S. Congress, was part of the reconstruction process. It is unconstitutional for anyone or any outside influence to force a state government, in any way, to add or take away or even to change one word within their state's constitution. This part should be stricken from the letter and become void from the time that it was written.

What about the territories that belong to the Confederate States? When it comes to something like this, I would have to say that whosoever wins control over the land and all that is on it assumes ownership as the most powerful country. However, once these territories become sovereign states they no longer belong to anyone other than themselves. As far as I know, these states are now voluntary members in the Union.

I have heard that the state of West Virginia is being called an outlaw state. Can this be a true statement; and if so, why? If you study the constitution of the United States and the constitution of the Confederate States, you will learn that the federal government and the presidents of both countries have no constitutional authority to create a state within a state, nor even to divide a state into separate parts. This is what the former president of the United States did with the state of Virginia. Moreover, that president was Mr. Abraham Lincoln. Let us not forget that Abraham Lincoln has never been the president over the Confederate States, especially the state of Virginia. West Virginia is a part of the state of Virginia; and the government of West Virginia, including that government's constitution and state song, etc. should not be recognized by the federal governments of the Union and of the Confederacy. Nor should they be recognized by any state government of the Confederacy and of the Union, not even to have business transactions, for the government of West Virginia is unconstitutional. The government of West Virginia must disband itself and once more unite itself as Virginians with Virginia. The state of Virginia has been divided into two parts, just as has been done with the Country of Germany. Let us embrace our southern brothers and sisters of West Virginia, for tyranny has divided them from us for far too long.

But my family has served under the American flag for generations, what about that? The same is true about my family. My family has served in the Army, Navy, and the Air Force of the United States of America. However, it doesn't change a thing. My family has been just as reconstructed as any other family here within the Confederacy and the Union. Every Country that falls under the subjection of an Empire shall, in time, accept that Empire as being their own. In addition, they will fight under that Empire's banner and for the benefit of that Empire. They will become transformed in order to fit within the system of that Empire. This is the other part of reconstruction, which I hope you're able to understand. I should also remind you that none of the U.S. banners has a copyright in order to be classified, in a separate category, as an American flag. All National banners of every Country, from the top of North America to the bottom of South America, are indeed an American Flag.

But if we are not legal members in the Union, then what responsibility does the Union federal government have to us? Since we are subjects, and in the service of the Empire, the only moral responsibility or obligation that the Yankee Empire has is the protection of her work force, which are people of the Confederacy. However, the Yankee Empire has done a poor job in that simple task. They allowed German submarines to stalk our eastern shores during the second grand war. Too many Confederates and Yankees die while transporting supplies to Great Britain. This was done in order to help Great Britain with the War effort.

We must not let our emotions and our decisions, that are based on past ignorance, to cloud our minds and to compromise our ability to look at things more clearly. Moreover, to take any issue apart in order to compare it to other possibilities, we must trust that the truth shall always come forward and stand on its own, providing that all evidence is brought forward in the presence of our people. With all of the evidence and the information before us, and requesting wisdom from our Heavenly Father, we shall be able to make better choices in life, which shall affect our people and our Country. It shall also have an effect in our relationships with all of our neighboring Countries throughout this world. We must discipline our emotions, for our emotions can deceive us at times and become our worst enemy instead of our ally. Satan has, from the very beginning of this rebellion, been using human emotions as a weapon in order to destroy the very image of God. He is just as much the Father of Empires as he is the Father of Lies. That is just my personal opinion; however, God does not want those that have rejected Him to rule over His people – not in the Old Testament and definitely not in the New Testament. The situation between who is Master and who is servant is the same situation that exists between God and Satan and between the State government and the Federal government. They are kindred spirits. There is a connection between how man shall conduct himself and establish his Country, as it shall be from the influence of the spiritual war between good and evil and the final fate in his journey to either Heaven or Hell.

We must bring it to an end and allow this no more. For far too long the Yankee Empire has lied to us and led our Confederate people in any direction of their own choosing. While they make us keep one eye closed, they allow us only to see what they want us to see with our other eye. Indeed, is it not they who cling to the words of liberty and justice in the name of the Yankee Empire? However, they are also deciding whether or not other countries have that same right. Are their policies based on the foundation and the principles that were established by our Founding Fathers? If the graves were to give up their dead, and all of the political leaders of the United State were put on trial for treason with our Founding Fathers as the jury, what do you think the verdict would be? I believe that there would most likely be the grandest hanging part in all of North America, with the political leads as welcome guests. I ask you, have they not desecrated the ideas and sacrifices of our Founding Fathers, that were made by those who fought and died under their leadership? How many times must our Founding Fathers be required to roll over in their graves before the people of the United States wake up and have a revelation? How much clearer does the writing on the wall need to be? Yes! A great tragedy has taken place and the whole world has lost out. The Republic of the United States is no longer present to be a reflection for the whole world to look upon and strive to have for themselves. The evolutionary cycle of the ideas of the growing and transforming of our liberty within a Republic has been trampled upon since the federal government of the Confederate States of America was overthrown.

Once the United States had overthrown the Confederate States a horrific statement was being made, in an indirect way, to the whole world. That statement is this: *Liberty is not what was meant by our Founding Fathers. It is whatever we desire it to be at the very moment we desire to use it. It is not for anyone who embraces the foolish ideas of our Founding Fathers. Liberty is we, of the Federal government. We shall distribute what powers and liberties we desire to distribute to the people who are faithful to us.* In truth, they are saying that liberty belongs to those who have the power to rule over the very people that they were meant to serve. Abraham Lincoln and all the political vampires that have served the centralist Mafia, from his time to the present, have been recognized by the whole world as hypocrites. For they have made a mockery out of the very documents that brought true liberty to our understanding. The question is: where will this end and what shall be the fate of our people in the near future? Are we going to continue to live our life as mindless chattel? I ask you not to allow this to go on any longer. When it comes to our people, we must be gentle, yet firm and direct, about our true Nationality. We must not be too quick to condemn anyone who continues to embrace this American illusion. All we can do is share the real information of our history to our people and hope that they are open minded enough to compare the evidence and accept the truth for themselves. A time will come when our creator shall restore our freedom for our Country. As that time does come, those who are bringing up the rear and still clinging to their U.S. citizenship shall be relocated o the United States borders. The Governments of the Confederate States and of the United States will work together and help each other with the transactions of those who are loyal to the Union and those who desire state citizenship in the Confederacy.

I have questioned myself about why it was necessary to go all the way in destroying the government of the Confederate States on the ground of treason, yet never bringing those people forward and putting them on trial for committing such a crime. Surely they are not stupid enough to believe that their war was supposed to settle this issue. If this had been brought to trial, with a neutral courtroom and all of the evidence brought forth and heard throughout the world, then the truth would have been forever settled. I find it strange that the United States had a conviction strong enough to make war upon us and force us back into the Union without proof of this treason that has been added to our ancestors' history. If this court was open to the public, did not take either side, and let the facts speak for themselves, then the struggle over the subject would not be coming back. If it was proven, in a court of law, that any state is not able to leave the Union and that the Confederacy is unconstitutional, then the final nail would have been placed in the coffin of the Southern cause. She would have been buried forever, never to be remembered.

If the verdict had gone the other way, and the United States was proven to be in the wrong, then the Union forces would have had to remove themselves from our Confederate soil and recognize the sovereignty of the Constitution of the Confederate States of America. The first step in Democracy would have been crippled. In addition, the States of the Union might have risen up and taken control of their federal government. The constitution of the United States would have been saved, and the people of the Union would not so quickly play the role of the puppet for their federal government. Moreover, this is the very reason that the Confederate leaders could not have their day in court. If the United States was proven to be in the wrong, the ability of the Federal government to gain more power over the States of the Union would have been jeopardized. If the Confederacy had won the war or the battle in court, then, in truth, the Union would have been saved. The Constitution of the United States would once more be restored to its true form and put back under the control of the States of the Union. This would protect the sovereignty of the State governments of the Union and give them less desire to leave the Union, unlike the way it is at the present time. If you were to leave the Union now, there would not be much left of our people or of your State. Nevertheless, please remember that it was in our constitution of the Confederate

States that we asked for the blessing of our creator and not of the United States. It would be great if the United States would recognize that we are a separate Country; however, it is not required that they do so. In fact, it does not matter if the United States refuses to give us its blessings because we can just as easily live without them.

I do not know who made this statement; however, someone once said, *"Democracy is Lucifer's most effective and most subtle form of imitation of government"*. I truly do hold this statement to my heart. In fact, this is clearer and more understandable than my writing of an entire book. Once the Union forces have removed themselves from our Nation, all we have to do is pick up where we left off during their invasion. It is not necessary for us to secede once more. The first time was constitutional and could not be constitutional the second or third time. The only problem that we will have is this: overcoming the growing stages of the definition of the Republic. If the United States had not invaded us in the past, this problem would already be behind us now. This is what I call the *Evolutionary cycle of ideas for our Republic*. Indeed, it was the United States that gave birth to the Republic. Nevertheless, the Confederate States were teaching this Republic to become a toddler. After the invasion had destroyed the government of the Confederacy, the federalists had to step in, to stunt the growth of the Republic, and to keep it in its infant stage. The Republic has never left her cradle since that time; and she will not, not until we are a free people once more. May God bring that day to us soon!

Passing The Buck

It would seem that all of the problems that are present in the Confederacy in our present time are either directly or indirectly being blamed on the Confederate States government. Segregation and the using of all flags of the Confederacy for the purpose of white power. The murders of our Confederate Negroes, by those with feelings of hatred, and the white uprising during the social or civil rights movement. But for the sake of reasoning, I should clear this up. Every time the Yankee Empire gives their stories about the injustice toward the Confederate Negroes, it always starts with the evil Confederacy during the war. It is as if they're saying that this was a war, not about state rights and the liberties of the state governments, but a war over racial issues and one race keeping the other race down. Once the Confederate States government was dispersed, the Confederacy was at the mercy and tyranny of the United States government. The Confederate States government has had many people of different races who fought for the Confederate cause. Therefore, if the federal government of the Confederacy had been present, they would not approve nor defend any of the Nations or States Banners to be used as symbols of white power or black power or for anything else, for that matter. The problems started with the act of war and continue with the present occupying and reconstructing of our people. This new south is neither the Confederate south nor the southern south. It is the new Yankee south. If the Confederate government were presently with us, they would look at things in a different light. The war had changed everything and everybody. The southern states would have phased out slavery and no one of any race would either own nor became a slave. The war had changed everything for everybody: the economy and the trade market, the issue about slavery and the new outlook and respect for all slaves that fought for the cause, and the personal views about the foreign Yankee invaders. Not only did they enslave us to their nation, they have enslaved us with their ideology and philosophy of life, including politics and their version of liberty. Their version of their reality, in short, is the cloning process of our Nation into theirs.

If our Confederate government had not been dispersed, I'm confident that they would have made some bad and poor policies from time to time; but since they were unable to do so, other people should not hold the Confederacy accountable for the ignorant opinions of others. The flag of our Confederacy does not belong to the hate groups' ideologies, so don't point your finger out of ignorance, toward our banners. Ignorant people are quick to sling hatred and opinions of bigotry toward our Confederate Nation and symbols and people, yet they have a sudden trauma of memory loss when it comes to the war crimes toward the world and the cruelty that the Union federal government used toward their own citizens and toward Dixieland. They are quick to say that we should stop living in the past, yet they don't even know their own past, nor do they want to be reminded of anything bad therein. In reality it is they who are living the past, because they can't tell the difference between a Union of the Republic and the Union of Democracy. They still even celebrate the 4 of July as if nothing has changed since that time. I feel sorry for them, just as much as I do for my own people. Some people believe that it was necessary for the Confederate States to lose the war in order for the world war one and two to take place, so that these would lead up to the New World Order, thus fulfilling the Revelations of the bible. It's very possible that this may be true, but it doesn't change the fact of our true Nationality and our Nations Constitution. State rights, which is also the constitution of each State, is and always will be the sovereignty of each State. The only failure that the Government of the Confederate States committed, including its' military, is this: *They spent too much time giving themselves all the glory when they should have been giving it to our Lord God; and they spent too much time in backstabbing each other and caring for their own honor when they should be caring more for their people as a Nation and as a duty and responsibility as defenders of liberty.* As a true Republic and as Christians, we must not become the very reflection of our enemy. No matter who or what it may be. To rebel against evil in the spiritual and physical realm is a duty that falls upon all of our Confederate people.

Oh Tis The Sweet Land Of Liberty

The word "sovereignty" is a word that gives hope to those who embrace the ideas of liberty, just as it is a word that brings fear to those who desire to crush it. Sovereignty is the meaning of a free will to act in self-preservation, to protect and defend, and also to withdraw from that which could cause danger to all that is under its protection. It is a free will to act in one's ability as of being sovereign. To deny that sovereignty to someone or something is to deny that right to existence of self will.

This is what the Yankeenite Jacobins have been claiming in order to establish their Democracy, for it as they that claimed that the "States have never been free" and that it was the Federal Government which created the States all along. This philosophy is not only to crush the free will of permanently withdrawing oneself from others, but to break and override the Constitutions of the sovereign State governments. Once the State Governments have been put into submission unto the federal government, then the federal Constitution becomes null and void. This is true due to the fact that the Federal Constitution is the Commandments of the Republic.

The Republic is designed to function under the sovereignty of the member States. Any other form of government has no submission unto the sovereignty of anything else. It was necessary to crush the Republic of the government of the Confederate States because it was the Southern states that held on to the ideas of the Republic from the Original Constitution of the United States. Once the Confederacy was put under the boot of Union rule, thus began the slow dismantling of the Union of the Republic to the present Union of Democracy. Remember this! The Confederacy had a lot of supporters from the Union States who felt the same about the ideas of our Founding Fathers and their Republic, not to mention the fact that they also recognized the Confederacy as a true Nation. The Confederate States had a strong influence and friends around the world, despite the fact that we were fighting to preserve the sovereignty of our Confederate Federal Constitution and States Constitutions.

Fate would have it like a collision at the intersection of moving vehicles, after Union troops were unconstitutionally sent into the State of South Carolina. Everyone from the Union wanted to jump on the war wagon and destroy and enslave the Southland. The abolitionist terrorists and the Jacobins, and let us not forget the support of the industrialism, could all smell the scent of power and profit in the air from the war movement. And now we are living in the times of the misconceptions of liberty and being an American, the illusions of Democracy and the materialism and secularism that go along with it. The very death cry of mankind as they shouted of liberty in the name of Democracy or Communism and Fascism: the three formulas that have plagued the present Confederacy and Union of this day. The very false illusion of being a good citizen is to shut up and pay your taxes and spend your money, and once in a while, to be sure to display the Federalist Banner.

Truth can be hidden from the public's eyes, but that's all you can do with the truth. Liberty begins with your State's Constitution, which establishes the sovereignty and independence of your Country or State; and by the sovereignty of the States, the Federal Constitution and government is born. One need sonly to look at and study the Declaration of Independence to see and understand that at the same time the States proclaimed their Independence was also the same time that they "the States" proclaimed the new federal government of the United States. But even after this statement was made, the States still had to ratify the Constitution of the United States of America. The purpose of the Federal Constitution is not only to regulate the powers of the federal government, but must work in agreement with the State Constitution and not as a form of a contradiction to the sovereignty of the Constitution of those said Countries or States. It was never the desire to create the federal government as a central power. Only the Federalist leaders wanted this. The anti-Federalists wanted a Republic and were able to convince the citizens of those States to support the idea. From 1776 to 1860 the United States was a government of the Republic and a Nation of sovereign States or Countries. But this great Republic was not able to stand up to the influence of the French Revolution and its mob rule. After the federal government of the Confederacy was dispersed near the end of the war, equality of Democracy from the French Revolution had replaced the Government of the Republic that was founded upon the Ten Commandments.

The Nation that once was is no more, for it had transformed or mutated into something different from what our Founding Fathers had established. Everything looks the same on the outside; but from within, everything is not.

This is what's causing such a grand deception to those who cannot understand why their rights are being violated everyday. We can safely say that the United States of America does not exist any longer, because the word United States (meaning more than one) is a clarifying of the government of the Republic. Now this bygone Nation has transformed into a Nation of Democracy or into the United State of America. The fact is that the government of the Republic must function within the Federal Constitution and with equal relations with all sovereign States. Being that the Democracy is now in place and all of the sovereign powers have now been transferred to the federal government, this is a clear case that the celebration of the fourth of July is in fact a celebration of a lost Nation and its liberty. However the Confederate States had never stopped being a separate Nation, because the government of the Confederate States of America was and still is a Republic: meaning that all powers still belong to the sovereign States of the Confederacy. Even with the dispersal of the federal government, the Southern States still have the sovereign power to restore and reestablish that same government; but if destruction were to fall upon the government of the United State and its democracy, then that National would no longer exist, because the whole concept and all of the sovereign powers were taken from the States and given to the Union federal government.

It is clear that under a Democracy the Declaration of Independence is invalid and that the Southern States would not be allowed to secede from the Union. Secession would be in violation of the concept of one unit and centralizing powers. The only requirement for our Confederate States to restore our federal government and to restore the sovereignty to our States is for the Union forces of the United State to withdraw peacefully from our Confederate borders. For most Confederates like myself, this is what we are hoping for; but if not , then we will have to wait and bring the case to our King Jesus when He returns to take His throne. The Jacobins believe that once the Confederate government had dispersed the Confederate States no longer existed as a Nation, because they had the idea of a centralizing government being the representation of our Nation. This is also false because as long as the Confederate States continued to have our Federal Constitution of the Confederate States of American then all that is required is to reestablish the federal government of the Confederacy. Since the States of the Confederacy had constitutionally seceded from the Union and have never constitutionally seceded from the Confederacy and then rejoined the Union, this is clear evidence that we are not more part of the United States of the Republic than we are part of the United State of Democracy.

Presently the States of the south could not constitutionally join the Union because of the fact of the presence of the influence of the federalist Jacobins within the State governments and the fact that the Confederate States is not able to act in a sovereign way without the fear and loyalty to the Yankeenite Empire. The State governments must first rediscover their true identity as Confederates before they are able to make a moral and a Constitutionally correct move in deciding to leave the Confederacy and rejoin the Union. It is true that at the present our Confederate people are citizens of the United State, not because it's constitutional, but because of the fact of the present Union military forces that are occupying our Nation. Under a Republic the citizens of the Union would be member citizens of the States in which they live and the State in which they pay taxes. The same would be true for the citizens of the Confederacy in which they live. The so-called U.S. citizen is in reality a citizen of the government of Democracy and is not truly protected under their State and federal Constitutions. As I have said before, the smoke screen is used in order to transform the people and allow them to feel a sense of security and safety, while all the time believe that their Country is their federal government.

Another error is in believing that the Confederate States could not exist as a Nation without the approval of the government of the United State. It was after the war that the United State proclaimed that the Confederate States was not a Nation; but when the United States wrote the Declaration of Independence, nothing was written within it that was requesting the approval of the government of the United Kingdom to recognize them. To be truthful, the United States could care less if Great Britain ever gave their approval. So why should the Confederate States feel any differently? In fact, it was not the Confederate States that wanted to make war against the Union or to overthrow their government. It was not the Confederate States who originally invaded the Union first; and if the Union wanted to Constitutionally do away with slavery, then the Confederate States would not care what they did within their own borders.

Where in the Holy Bible does it give any government or Nation the authority to decide who has the right to approve or disapprove of another Nation being formed? I have not found the answer to that one yet; but one thing is clear: the Confederate States did not and was not required to fight for Independence. The Confederacy did not fight the same kind of war as the colonial war was. The Confederacy was fighting to preserve the Independence that the colonial war had won, and that was to preserve the Independence of the States, which the Declaration of Independence was talking about. The Declaration of Independence was not just a statement of liberty, but pertained also to the sovereignty of States and of the federal government. The federal Constitution is and always has been the limitation of the sovereignty of powers of the federal government. Why do you think that the United State and Briton were so quick to rescue France from the vise grips of the Nazis during World War II? It was because it was France that had given birth to the politics of "Democracy"! But let us take this a step further and see where it will lead us. Under the Federal Constitutions of the Confederate States and of the United States, it would be illegal for the federal governments to join or become an equal member with the United Nations or any other Nations or organizations, for this would violate the security and sovereignty of the federal Constitutions of both Nations and those that both governments are to uphold and enforce. It would also put the States' Constitutions in harm's way. It would be unconstitutional for the Nation's President to use military forces in action of war in other Countries without a declaration of war from Congress. The phrase "Peace enforcements" is used to bypass the federal Constitution. It is unconstitutional for the president to use military troops on the civilians of member States in order to violate the will of the people and to enforce social engineering upon the people.

It would be unconstitutional to allow the borders, including the ocean boundaries, to go unchecked and allow harm to anyone within the boundaries of those States. It would be unconstitutional to forbid any State from acting within its sovereign right to vote them out of that Nation. It would also be a violation to vote anything into the State and federal Constitutions that would be a contradiction to that which has been written within that Constitution. The only way to amend the State and federal Constitutions is upon the condition that whatever is added to the Constitution will not violate the basic rights of the States and the citizens of those said States. We do understand that during the times of changes the federal Constitution must be readjusted from time to time, but only in ways that do not violate the basic rights of sovereignty to those States. However, under a government of Democracy, anything goes, without checks and balances. All of these things have already taken place; and it was done under the government of a Democracy.

In reality, this war has never ended. The government of the Confederate States never did sign a peace treaty, nor did they sign a declaration of surrender to the United States government. The present military bases on Confederate soil and the reconstruction of brainwashing in public schools, the cultural genocide of the history and identity of our Confederate people, and the fact that the States can no longer have their own militia and guard their own borders testify to that. These are further evidence of a democracy in action. And let us not forget the taxation without representation in full swing. It is very gullible for anyone to believe that whoever wins the war is always in the right and set the final conclusion to all constitutional issues that are at hand. All that has even been proven is that, in history, all Empires are and always have been bullies and evil toward liberty for all of mankind. For as long as our Confederacy is under the vise grip of the Union, our fate will suffer the same evils. There never has been any other form of government of man that is superior to a Constitutional form of a Republic. The only form of government that is superior to a Constitutional Republic is the coming government with the head establishment of Christ Jesus. Let us pray our case to Christ and let Him deal with the distress of our beloved Confederacy.

Neo-americans

The syllable *Neo* represents something that is new or something that is different. For example, you've heard term Neo-Confederates or Neo-Nazis; but this is a poor classification and identification of the real subject at hand. The name Confederate is a much older title than the word American or Nazi. The word Confederate is a classification of a person who is from the Confederacy or of the Confederate States of America. The word Nazi is the classification of a person who believes in the ideology of fascism. A Nazi could be anyone from any Nation within the world; and it is foolish to believe that one can crush the ideology with an act of war. There is nothing Neo about the Nazis. The word *American* was given to the Yankees by one of the European Nations during world war one; but I don't remember which nation at this moment, in order to classify them separately from the rest of the Europeans. The word *American* is poor terminology because it only describes the continent of all of America North, South, and Central. You can say that you're an American and still not be telling what Nationality you are.

If I were to say that this person is Asian, you still would not know from what Nation this person came. If I were to say that this person was from Africa or South Africa, you would still not know from what Nation this person came. If I were to say that this person is European, what Nation would I be talking about? Right! It could be any of them. It is really selfish and self-centered for Yankees to believe that only they could be real Americans and everyone else from the American continent is not. By the same token, if I were to say that this person is Spanish am I also telling you this person's Nationality? The answer would be *No*. We have been proclaiming ourselves as being Americans for years now; but we have been doing it out of plain ignorance. The truth is that we are still Confederates and the Yankees are still Yankees; and that, my friends, will never change.

People have been pre-conditioned to believe that only the Unied State is *American* and its' Federalist National Flag is the only *American Flag*. However, in truth, all Nations and Countries or States that are within the American continent are Americans, just as every National and State flag from the Continent of America would be considered as being an American Flag. No one Nation has the copyright to the Title of *being an American or from America* and even though everyone knows the American nickname is directed toward the United State, it is still wrong and a false description of a Nation. Our founding and Confederate Forefathers have never considered themselves Americans. If you were to ask our Founding Fathers what Nation they were from, their answer would be *The United States*. If you were to ask them what Country they were from, *each one would give you the name of the State in which they lived*.

The only time that you would see the word *America* is in the full title of the United States, meaning *The United States of America*; and this only gives you the description of the continent on which this Nation is located. The same goes for our beloved Confederacy. The Confederate States of America is a clear indication that the Confederacy is from the American continent. Words have meaning; and if you use the meaning in the wrong way, then you will change the concept of the meaning of the word. When you say that you are an *American*, you are taking the recognition away from your Nation. To say that you are an American is to deny the borderlines of each State and of every Nation, thus the word becomes transformed into a centralized concept. Let me share something else with you. What would it mean if someone were to say that they are *citizens of the world*? It would be a statement that denies the reality of all Nations of Earth. It is also the concept of a one-world government that the Holy Bible has spoken about. People will accept this idea of world citizenry just as quickly as they accept the idea of being an American.

Do you see the writing in the sand? Can you see the circle coming about? First we were all Countrymen of our State in which we live. Next, we are a Nation without State borders. Then we become as one throughout the whole continent. Then, finally, we are one throughout the whole world. Do I sound crazy to you? Then maybe you should spend more time in studying the Bible and world history, and compare it with the changes in our present history. Presently the people have not been conditioned to accept the idea of being citizens of the world; but maybe in a few generations more, they just might. What! You don't believe it can happen? It took less than one hundred years to transform the Yankees and the Confederates into believing that they are Americans. Who's to stop them now? What about the European currency? Doesn't this deny the sovereignty of the Nations of Europe? It sure does!

When the Yankees are speaking about freedom, it's not the same version of freedom that we believe in, at least not for most of them. They believe in the version of freedom in a Democracy. They believe that a Constitutional Republic is a outdated concept of liberty. If this wasn't true, then why haven't they had a Real Revolution in order to restore their Government of the Republic? We still believe in a Constitutional Republic; and that is why we know the difference between the two. What they call freedom is what we would call slavery, except for the scalawags, of course.

For us who know real history, the word Yankee would bring the same feelings as the word Nazi would bring to the Jewish Nation. The Confederate Holocaust is a part of history to which the Yankees would never admit. In fact, the Nazis also denied the truth of killing the Jews after the war; but they did pay for their war crimes because they had lost the war. The Yankees didn't lose the war against us; and therefore, they never went to trial for their war crimes against our Confederate People (and I'm including every Confederate of race that came across the Federalist troops. The Yankees back home never really knew what their troops did to our people. Anyone who stood up to the invasion by this foreign force of the United State was crushed under the boots of their troops. To be truthful, their freedom is killing us; and it's being done without firing a shot. Take a look at us now and compare us to the way were back then. Look at what we are becoming, too.

A Yankee Jew, with whom I work, has told me that since we lost the war, we should get over it and stop living in the past. He also said that we should take the Confederate battle flag down and forever keep it down. I did not reply to his comment because I wanted to see how much he knew and understood about the subject. The question I would like to ask is this: The Confederate holocaust took place long before the German Jews' Holocaust. Should we also forget the Jewish holocaust as well? Even though it was the Confederate soldier that served under the U.S. banner to free the Jews from the Nazis' prisons? Why should we deny our Birthright as a people and as a Nation just because the Yankee Empire wants to brush it under the rug and not deal with it nor make it right with us? And why should we continue to trust their form of education about what they say we are and what took place? Why should we trust them on anything?

When the Native Indians quoted the statement about the Great White Father (United States Government) speaking with a forked tongue, they weren't just whistling Dixie. Even to this day, we need to "take it with a grain of salt" in everything this government says and everything in which they are involved. You can never be sure what may or may not be true.

As for the flag, I say this: Fly the Federalist Empire Banner on Federalist buildings only and let them not be concerned about what we do with our true peoples' flags. But let me get back to the first subject. The information below would be a far more proper and truer answer to claim.

TABLE OF IDENTIFICATION

I am from the: Confederate States of America   United State of America

                    Confederate State of   United State of
                    _____   _____

NAME THE STATE WHERE YOU LIVE

I am a citizen of the: Confederacy   Union

                           Confederate State of   United State of
                           _____   _____

NAME THE STATE WHERE YOU LIVE
[COMMENT]: The citizenship of the Confederacy would be true after the peaceful removal of the Federal Union forces. Until then, we are citizens of the Yankee Empire, just as other Nations that were under the rulership of the Roman Empire.

The Confederate Spirit

With a vision and hope/
> To dream and lay out hopes within a prayer/ We've laid down our arms/
> And cast our cares to the front of the cross/ As we pray to Christ for Liberty and justice/
> That he shall not have forgotten us, and our Southern cause/ Amen and Amen/

The greatest loss is not just by having the liberty and the freedom of a people and Nation taken away and controlled at all times, but, as a people, it is also to lose hope and to dream no more. The final blow to seal our fate as a people is to lose vision and faithfulness to our creator and his son. We the Confederate people are of many different races and our ancestors are from many different Nationalities. Yet we live on the same land and have fought side by side when danger came to our door. We share the same heritage and cultures that makes the identify of our Southern Confederacy. We worship the one and only GOD and his SON. We have a connection that united us to stand together as many countries and to stand together as a Nation for the same hope and dreams and rights as a people that was mentioned in the Declaration of Independence. As a Nation and as a people, we have been be beaten and robbed and thrown into slavery. Union shackles have been put, not upon our hands and feet, worse yet, upon our minds and hearts.

Before changes can take place around us, they first must take place within us. As a Nation, we must be able to stand in front of our God and be held accountable for all of our government's deeds. As a people, we must cling to the race and righteousness before we are standing in the presence of our Creator. We as a people must at all times be conscious of our actions and how we are relating to each other, and we should not let foreign National governments establish changes in our society. We as a people must solve our own problems in the ways that will not conflict with the teachings of our Lord Christ Jesus and not violate anyone's constitutional rights as citizens of the Confederate States of America. Self-searching from the heart is something we must strive for in our everyday life. Let us strive to grow more spiritually, emotionally, mentally, and financially, for our lives will ends as quick as a breath and may affect those that we leave behind.

We need to read more books and watch less television and self-educate ourselves. We must question everything that we have learned and compare it with other information and ideas, for it was God Jehovah who gave us a mind with which to think and understand. We must become self-sufficient and relearn our home crafts of gardening, cooking, quilt and clothing making. We need to relearn the hunting skills that were once handed down from generation to generation. We need to be independent and not rely upon the Yankee economics and their Wall Street. Technology must be put in its proper place and not be depended upon fully. In poverty and war, we as a people and as a sovereign Nation, must once more relearn self-sufficiency. We must also learn to care for the Earth that God has put in our care.

We also need to relearn and teach family values once more. We must remove ourselves from the thought control of the reconstruction camps (public schools) of the United State government and establish home schools for all of our people, from this day forward. We need to defend and support our States constitutions and work to restore our true National constitution of the Confederate States of America. Instead of flying every flag of the Confederacy, let us focus on our final constitutional National flag and fly that alone (Our Third National). We must regain control over all forms of media and educational resources within our Confederate borders. We must work to restore our Republic of our State governments before we can ever hope to restore our National government of the Confederate Status. Until that time, we must give our taxes to the Union, but at no time believe everything that we hear from them (a grain of salt). We should not at any time give them our trust or support or our devotion. We should give the Union our prayers and remind them of the foundation of their Nation and of the birth right of ours, but nothing more. We must establish a new cinema studio here in Dixie Land, giving it the duty and the responsibility to promote pro-Christian and family films. It should also promote pro-Confederate and true historical films as well.

We must regulate the quality of films' artwork and the garbage films of Hollywood and ban all garbage films from being imported into our borders. We must make war on drugs and against any Nation that bring them into our Confederacy, because the bringing of drugs into our Nation is no different than a Nation's flying over and dropping bombs upon our citizens' homes. We must establish a university that will promote and teach arts and crafts; and should cover all of these areas:

1. painting
2. drawing
3. literature
4. cooking
5. fishing
6. hunting
7. gardening
8. music: southern rock, jazz, bluegrass, country, and classical, Christian music of many forms
9. and other forms of arts and crafts that are good for our society and survival

After our independence has been reestablished, we need an organization for our children that would be similar to Boy Scouts and Girl Scouts of North America. We should request that States to give a stated amount of money to NASA and forbid our National government from getting involved. NASA should have the authority to do business with anyone as long as it does not violate the safety and sovereignty of the Confederacy and does not cause harm to our world. NASA should have a policy that stries for the betterment of mankind and not be used in the war of politics. Nor should NASA ever be used as a weapon of war. We, too, as a people should have a dream: the hope and dream to be a free Republic of Dixie once more. But that is not enough, for that dream must go further beyond our independence as a people and a Nation; and we must strive to improve ourselves as individuals and as a people. We must not become stagnated and stale.

We must follow the footsteps of not only our Lord Jesus Christ, but the footsteps of our Founding

Fathers and their ideology of independence. The ability to stretch our abilities and to see what we can do and what we can learn and how to overcome. It is not good enough to become the best at one thing or to limit ourselves to the four corners of our mind. We are explorers of not only ourselves, but of that which is beyond the imagination of thought. We can never put our hopes and dreams inside a treasure chest and bury it in the back of our minds, hoping that some day it shall all fall into its' proper place. We must also take that chance of failure and learn from our mistakes, because that too is a small portion of the meaning of being free. We must also be willing to lose everything that belongs to us and even our lives in order to protect our independence as a Nation and as a people, just as our Confederate Ancestors once did for themselves and for their future generations. Our lives shall pass us by as quickly as a blink of an eye, and they shall not return to us for corrections.

The greatest thing about freedom is to understand that it can be as easily lost as the sudden death of someone that you love; and what you will do and how you will live your life with that gift can affect your personal life and the lives of those who come in contact with you. We can only hope that as long as we are faithful to our true Creator and to our family and country that our lives have not been lived in vain. In the end it is our Creator who determines the value of his creations.

All Hail Caesar!

Like a Greek God, he sits upon his throne within his temple and looks across the land as if he is all-seeing and the all-knowing. His own Nation has crowned him as the *Father of Democracy*, while some of the Confederate Americans have given him the title of *The American Caesar.* Another title that describes him would be *The North American Emperor.* That Lincoln Memorial across the Potomac River is the symbol of a new nation that has rejected its original foundation and is no longer the Nation that had been founded. It has become foreign and alien to the nation that our Founding Forefathers had established. And just as their decedents, they would have stood under our States and our Confederate National banner and fought against it. But now, a statue of this dictator with his son has been placed on the grounds of our Liberty's Capital of the Confederate States. Now the sweet land of Virginia has an image of a foreign nation's president forever present in Richmond.

His Nation keeps reminding us that they had to enslave our Confederate Nation in order to set us free. This is the same propaganda that the Communist Nations like to proclaim; and the sad part about it is that they really do believe this stuff. But how can we believe that we are truly free? For if we were free then it wouldn't have been required for us to withdraw our States and form a new Nation. If we were truly free, then our people would have not been required to fight against that nation's banner that was once theirs. If we were truly free, we wouldn't be living under the yoke of its Democracy. If we were truly free, then their Nation's Banner would not be flying on our Nation's soil. I must be bold about this; and I'm only speaking for myself personally. Nothing has changed from that time when they had invaded our sovereign States. It's that same government, that same Nation, that same national banner. in fact, they have become much worse. We would like to believe that by some mysterious chance that nation has repented of their sins and now they have returned to their original origins as a Nation of George Washington past. But this has never been close to the truth.

More than 50,635 Confederate Americans (men, women, and children) suffered and died because of this American Emperor. More than 50,635 Confederate Americans had fallen in blood because of his Nation. And the blood of these Confederate Americans is upon his Nation's banner. His government supported the war crimes and the Confederate Holocaust that was done under his command; and it was he who created a division in his Nation. A White supremacist and a segregationist including being an atheist doesn't seem to be important to that Yankee Nation. 10,000 Native Confederate Americans; 5,000 Hispanic Confederate Americans; 3,500 Hebrew Confederate Americans stood in defense of their States Constitutions, including the defense of their Nations constitution of the Confederate States. Chinese and Polish Confederate Americans did their part also. Irish, Scottish, English and German Confederate

Americans marched in the name of liberty. And let us not forget the brave African Confederate Americans of free and of slaves that would not allow strangers from a strange land to make war upon their home land of Dixie.

These are the true American Patriots, for they are the symbol of *The Sons and Daughters of Liberty*. In the name of freedom and liberty, the United States invaded our land and our homes and our Nation to spill our people's blood. They burned our people's homes and crops and they killed any livestock that they could not take. They raped and murdered and pillaged in the name of their own righteousness. The United States had initially starved our Confederate *prisoners of war* in their death camps when they could easily clothe and feed their own troops and civilians. Yet they try to play the propaganda game as though it was they that were the victim and that it was we who divided and caused them to no longer be a Nation. In my heart, could I fly the stars and stripes and pledge their Allegiance now that I know the truth of all this? As a Christian and as a Confederate I could not. We did not lose the war because were in the wrong. We lost the war because we had stumbled over our own pride and lost our focus on God who was with us in times of battle. For God is not a politician, and only in righteousness and faithfulness is the path of His love. All He ever asks from us is to be the same to Him.

While the cultural cleansing is taking place toward our Confederate people and Nation, it is clear that the majority of our indoctrinated people does not realize nor care either way. With the removal of everything that defines us as a separate people and Nation, it seems that now those foreign Yanks may be working on replacing all this with their own Yankee version: remove this Confederate statue and replace it with a Yankee statue. Our Confederate identity is the evidence that their so-called civil War is based on lies and propaganda. Our people have become so brainwashed and stupid that they will mock and put down other Confederates in other Southern States just because they talk more southern or speak with a deeper southern accent. They are so ashamed of being classified as a redneck or hillbilly that they believe that only those Yankees are truly speaking the real proper English. Our people have become so ignorant and naïve that they can be directed in any direction, like a dog on a leash.

Their Yankee version of their so-called civil war is such a contradiction and is consistently changing in order to lay on the emotions that it all amounts up to a pile of horse manure. Sometime it can get so knee deep that it makes you nauseated. I grow so tired, at times, in listening to all of their mind control methods, because it all mounts to a bunch of rubbish. The Yankees have learned long ago that it is just as effective to control the minds of the people as it is to control them by bayonet; and to control the people, you must have control over the education of history and the peoples' identity, as well as the spiritual beliefs. It's a weapon that takes generations to show its effectiveness, but in the end it will cause the people to freely become a loyal and submissive majority most of the time.

It appears that regardless of the amount of evidence of our historical truth, it seems that they (the Yanks) and the socialist liberals continue to ignore our side and play on the words of emotions in order to keep us sidetracked. They don't care about the truth; and they don't care about us. That is just a plain fact. We, the unreconstructed Confederates, have become the minority in our society because we don't have control over our people's communication and education systems. With this fast-paced society as it is, we know that most people don't read real books anymore. Therefore we must use more modern methods to reach out and educate our Confederate Nation on the real truth. We know that constitutionally that flag of abomination of the United State does not belong anywhere on our Nation's soil. Not in our Nation's capitol and not over our people's hearts. I do believe that in order for us to embrace the National banner of the United State we must be willing to condemn the actions of our Confederate ancestors. We must be willing to denounce the very ideology of our Founding Forefathers and the meaning of the Declaration of Independence of the United States. We must be willing to approve the immoral decisions and actions of the policies that that government has approved. We must also be willing to deny the right of ourselves to be a separate Nation. We must be willing to submit to their rule so that we could call ourselves free under their Democracy. We must be willing to be their chattel and do their bidding. The national banner of the United State is a flag that is a symbol of evil and tyranny. The liberties of our people and the innocents of Native Indian women and children have fallen under their actions of genocide. I, in good conscience, could not embrace this banner as most of my people have.

The thing that we fail to remember is that we are the by-products after the war. We are the people after the fact. We do not remember what it was like to have a foreign Nation to invade us; but our ancestors do. We do not know the freedoms that our ancestors had and therefore we cannot say that we re truly free. If we are truly free, then what kind of freedom were our people fighting for? If we do not have the freedom of our ancestors, then what kind of freedom do we really have? For it we were truly free, then it would not have been required for us to leave the Union in the first place; and our people would not be required to fight and die in our defense. Let us remember this! Our ancestors fought in the defense of the understanding of the liberties of our Founding Forefathers; and those liberties that they were fighting for were meant to be handed down to us. When they went into battle, it was for our future that they were trying to preserve. The one thing that we have tried to teach these damn Yankees, the very lesson that we are starting to forget, is this: *The point of a bayonet cannot settle the outcome of the truth.*

The teachings of the United State version of their civil war is nothing more than a Yankee's version of a Trojan horse, because it is based on halftruths and censorship of history. In all honesty, we cannot honestly say that the free Confederate Negroes or that the Native Confederate Indians are better off now under the rulership of this foreign Nation of the United State and of its Democracy no more than we could say that they wouldn't have been better off without the protection of the constitutional Republic of our Confederate States. Nor should we be gullible enough to believe that we have more freedom than our ancestors once had. We as a people must come to the reality that we have become enslaved by the military power and of the propaganda or, if you like, the indoctrination of the United State. We are dying as a Nation, as a people, and as a race. And I'm not just talking about one particular race of people. It is imperative that we set the flames to their Trojan horse. We must continue to burn this Yankee Trojan horse until it is totally consumed with fire.

We must gain control over as much of our education and communications as we are able. We must support home schooling in our home States and teach real Confederate American history. We must, as A People, as a Country, and as a Confederate Nation, be in good standing with the God of our Christ Jesus. We must relearn the good things and not the bad and hand them down to our future generations. Our heritage is something that we are to live by, not just something for us to only remember, for heritage is not just something that tells about us, it is the identity of ourselves as a people, as a Nation, and as individuals. The Hebrews have been persecuted for the fact of their Judaism and for the fact that they are Hebrews. We are being persecuted for being Christians and for the fact that we are Confederate Americans. Our Confederate American Heritage must be protected above and before all other foreign heritage and cultures, because all other forms of foreign culture are a contradiction to our Nation's and our people's identity. The reconstruction and assimilation of our people and Nation did not end after the unconstitutional war of the United States. The military war is over, however the cold war is still progressing toward their fulfillment of elimination or cultural cleansing toward our people and Nation of the Confederate States. It is even popular now for them to use our South land as a dump sight for their toxic waste.

Also, the diversity training is another program of this cultural cleansing. It is used to reject all that is Confederate American and is used to make us focus on every other people of cultures that have rejected our way of life in order to transform our Confederate Nation into something that is foreign. You will not find any sensitive training in the Union to enable the Yankees to understand and respect everything that defines us as Confederate Americans or, if you like, Southrons. In fact, Hell would freeze over before they would ever care about our rights and our feelings. As to the response to the Lincoln statue in Richmond, Virginia, CSA, what would you believe the reaction might be if we were to build a monument of the Great Seal of the Confederate States of America and place it in the Nation's Capitol of the United State? How about building a statue of John Wilkes Booth, and on the front shall be written *Death To Tyrants* and place it in the capital of Illinois USA. Or maybe we should have a statue of our First President: Jefferson Davis and place it in the United State Capitol with one of his speeches written on the bottom. This just might be a fair trade on both sides. What do you think?

Whos Lost Cause?

I'm sure that you have heard of the phrase *the Confederacy and the lost cause*; or you may have heard something that would be similar to that wording. I believe that this *cause* should have a better definition than what the Union Federalist would like for you to believe. They would like for you to believe that the southern cause was another form of colonial war that was required for the south to win in order to become a separate Nation apart from the United States. It's what the Yankees like to call a revolution; however, this is more false propaganda that would put fear in the hearts of the people and make it sound that since the south had lost the war the question of the independence of the southern States was settled. In reality none of this is true. The fact was that the Southern States had no desire or intentions to invade the Northern States. If it was true that the Southern States were required to win their independence then they would be the ones who had to act by invading the North. They would have to be willing to overthrow the government of the United States and they would not have waited four years later in the defense mode. It was finally out of desperation that they even invaded the United States at all.

The last thing that the Southern People wanted to do was to destroy the very dream that the Northern and southern Founding Forefathers had established: the very dream of true liberty that their Ancestors fought and bled for. If you were to study our Confederate history more deeply you would have to realize that as they were creating the Federal government, the Federal Constitution, the National or Great Seal, including the National Anthem, and let us not forget the peace treaties with the Native American Indians. Oh, I also would like to mention the Federal and State Currency and Navy and the State Militias. When all of this was done, it was done in a way as if they had already had the authority to do so. Everything was being done in a legal and constitutional manner. It would be a contradiction for them to fight for Independence, if it was required for them to destroy the Union. For if they were to do that, then they would have destroyed the very foundation of that Constitutional Republic.

Instead, they believe that they were already free and they were only acting on the rights that had been given to them by our Founding forefathers. Why would they want to destroy that Foundation of a Constitutional Republic when they would be turning around and placing the Confederacy right back on top of that Foundation? It would be stupid for them to do so. Instead, they were fighting to preserve their Independence that they had received from our Founding Forefathers. Therefore, the Southern cause that they were fighting for is the very ideology that gave them their Independence after the colonial war. In truth, it is the voice of Democracy that is saying that the Southern Cause is a lost cause, because it is the cause of our Founding Forefathers that they reject and condemn. Therefore, by directly condemning the Constitutional Republic of these Confederate States, they are indirectly condemning the constitutional Republic of that United States.

A Confederate Views:

The United States does not want the Confederate people to learn of their past. Ignoring the past is another form of justification for ignoring the facts that the past represents.

I could not and would not be able to embrace the Constitution of my people in The Confederate States of America without such emotional affection and without having the deepest respect and admiration for the Constitution and the Declaration of Independence of that United States of America.

They say that the pen is mightier than the sword, but I say unto you that without the sword of the people to continually reinstate those liberties that they have earned then that sword shall become useless toward their defense! And those words from that pen become a voiceless action, and that paper upon which those words have been written shall no longer have the value that it once had.

What is liberty to me? It is the rights that God has given us and His judgment that falls upon us after our deaths.

Life is strange, with its twists and turns. From the experience of its mysteries, we do learn from life.

Why does history always repeat itself? Because man is of sin; and in sin, the greed for power is within him.

We must never look at our Nation and compare the liberties that we have with the rest of the world, for that would always be nearsighted. Instead, we must look in the mirror of our own reflection, because true liberty never changes. We must accept the fact that if our reflection is not the same as that of our Founding Fathers, then, indeed, we are the ones who are in danger of tyranny and death!

The Theory of Evolution of Mankind is indeed nothing more than a theory; and theory is a word that is used when there is no explanation or when the facts are ignored. It is an answer that is a contradiction to the mythical ideals believed to be the truth, a situation in which the answer becomes a multiple choice.

By: Mar. John T.
Nall Salisbury, N.C.
3 August 1997

More Confederate Views:

1. Let it be said and let it be heard throughout this world:
   That our Confederate forefathers publicly proclaim that Almighty God is over the people and Nation of *The Confederate States of America* . And this was stated in the Constitution of The Confederate States. And from this day forward, I proclaim this on the behalf of my Confederate people, that Christ Jesus is the one and only true Messiah and King of Kings, and the rightful heir and ruler of The Confederate States and of its people! To be spiritually and physically free from the bondage of sin and tyranny! This is the real meaning and understanding of The Southern Cause.
2. If vengeance is best, when it's a dish served cold, then true justice must be best when it's a dish served piping hot with a glass of sweet tea on the side. It would be much more fulfilling.
3. American patriotism should never be glorified, but it should be remembered as a continuation that falls upon us at the time of our birth.
4. History is what establishes the reality of our identity of who and what we are and what we were meant to be as a Southern people.
5. It should be a question of how a Nation can justify its actions of war and victory, when the actions of that government are a contradiction to the documents that limit powers of authority over that government, as well as how that government can violate the rights and liberties of those free states that are no longer part of that country nor under the power of that country's government.
6. As the victors write the history books, one must remember that each coin has but two sides and that you must search the other side that the victors might have suppressed in order to make a just comparison or fill in the blanks, to see if one side is holding the truth or if the truth remains some place within the middle. For the one who controls that knowledge shall control the fate and the thoughts within the minds of the people; and that is where you might find the birth of tyranny.

John T. Nall
Salisbury, N.C.
11 May 1998

Printed in C.S.A.

Confederate Views

(Final Closing)

1. They say that ignorance is bliss. I'm not sure if this is a lie of the devil or just another Yankee version of reality. It could just be one and the same.
2. We have never had an American Revolution, for it was a colonial war for independence only. A Revolution occurs when the people rise up to overthrow their present structure of government. Another form of mob rules.
3. We have never had a Civil War, for it was a war between two sovereign Nations. One Nation had invaded the other. A Civil War occurs when you have two factions that are fighting one another in order to have control over the present form of government.
4. The so-called American Civil War was actually the Yankeenite war. The Yankeenite war is the Federalist version of the French or Jacobin war for centurial powers.
5. Ignorance has run rampant upon the Earth, like the fields of wheat that have fallen prey to the armies of Locusts.
6. To pledge your loyalty to the Democracy of the Yankeenite Nation will have the same results as planting seeds of liberty in quicksand.
7. Ignorance is not a blessing; it is the introduction into slavery.
8. The first step to maintain or to regain freedom is to learn and know your rights.
9. The public schools are a legacy from the Reconstruction period toward the people of the Confederate States of America. It is now being used toward the Federalist citizens themselves during the present time.
10. Is the Confederate States a true Nation? The answer is "Yes, it is!" The Confederate States did not stop existing just because our Federal Government had dispersed during the unconstitutional invasion of the Yankeenite Nation. It is the sovereign compact between the States that not only created the Constitution of the Confederate States, but also created the Federal Government. The present State Governments of the Confederacy are in fact Reconstruction Governments that are loyal and fearful to the Government of the United State. For this reason they do not represent the voice of the citizens of their said States. The Reconstructed State Governments cannot vote themselves out of the Confederacy. Only a Sovereign State Government can Constitutionally vote itself out of the Confederacy.
11. If almost every State were to leave the Union, or even the Confederacy and both Federal

Governments were eradicated, so long as you have two Sovereign State Governments keeping the Federal Constitution active they are, in fact, still a Nation.

12. The first sign of liberty being in jeopardy is when the federal Government starts to interfere with the internal affairs of the State Governments.
13. Fifty percent of the parent's teaching is toward their own child. The other fifty percent is the child learning on its own.
14. After the child has grown up and is no longer needing to be raised by the parents, the child should reach out to God and have God to finish teaching him or her the rest of the lessons of life.
15. To ponder the truth is to question one's own common sense.
16. To stand up for liberty is to stand in the way of the delusional version of liberty.
17. To seek perfection is to live in the footsteps of Christ Jesus.
18. Fear is the creator of failures and mistakes.
19. Reality is only based upon the realm within our beliefs and its boundaries.
20. In reality we have a very think line between fate and good luck.
21. Constitutional liberty is a true liberty that never crosses over its boundary lines.
22. The first step to becoming free is to overcome one's ignorance of the truth.
23. The first step in defending our liberty is to always keep your powder dry and your gun loaded.
24. The first step in becoming a patriot is to defend and preserve your States or Countries Constitution. The second step is to defend and preserve your Federal Constitution of your Nation.
25. Liberty is like a reflection in a mirror, the same image of the foundation that was established by our Founding Fathers and from the influence of the great "I AM". The same great "I AM" who influenced our Confederate forefathers. Liberty cannot be compared to the freedom of the Nations in this World. That would be like comparing Apples to Oranges.
26. To know one's destiny is not always in knowing what must take place in order to reach that destination., but to put our trust in the Lord, that He will get us there. Leave the rest of the details to Him.
27. Anyone who is without faith in Christ Jesus is like a person who has been swept away by the rough currents of the river. The current that will lead them to their death that is just below the waterfall. Despite the failures in clinging to everything that drifts by. They still refuse to grab hold of the one who is reaching out to them.
28. There are two ways of sharing the good news of the Gospel: to share it and then to live within it.
29. Every door that you find along your journey of life has exits, which lead to different pathways. Once you let that door close before you, it will usually never open again. Be careful not to lock the wrong door behind you.
30. They that fear the truth of history feel safer in the delusional life that they call reality of false truths.
31. An individual's philosophy can only hold value to one's self and to those who have been influenced by it, for as long as that philosophy has the foundation of truth to it.

32. Philosophies have no bases of foundation if they are founded on the assumptions and the theories of ideas.
33. To assume is to allow error into a person's search for the truth and to hope that this assumption shall someday come true.
34. A philosophy has no meaning and purpose if it is not a way of life to those who believe in it.
35. "If the price I must pay for my freedom is to acknowledge that the government was granted the power to infringe on them, then I am not free." (By: Pol Anderson)
36. It is only by the Grace of God and the blood of Christ that I can proclaim myself as being a righteous Man, for without them I was doomed to death before I ever was born.
37. One of the greatest enemies of the support for our Southern Heritage and for the movement of restoring the Independence of our great Confederacy would be the censorship in the news media.
38. Yes, it's true. I'm one of those Bible thumping trailer trash that your mother had warned you about. Now, would you like to hear the good news of the Gospel?
39. Yes, it's true! I am that bible thumping trailer trash that your Yankee family had warned you about. Now, would you like to hear the good news of the Gospel?
40. It was he! Ronald Reagan, the former president of the United State, that was our modern day version of George Washington. He is the living proof that a man does not always have to be perfect to always be great. He has our deepest respect and admiration. May our Lord God care for and bless him and his family.
41. The duty of a Christian is not to have hatred toward anyone, but to hate the sins and the destruction of all of the creator's creation that is caused by Mankind. For we cannot have Christ within us when we are filled with hate. And if Christ were not in us, then what good would it be for Christ to be with us?
42. History is the telling of the world's truthful past.
43. A man who is without character is someone who is not, by definition, a real Man.
44. A Man who is forgiving, willing to admit his mistakes, and willing to apologize, is the kind of Man who deserves your respect.
45. While the Yankees are busy pointing their fingers at the speck that is in the Confederate eyes they should be more concerned with the plank that is in their own eyes. The teachings of Christ are good enough for anybody.
46. One should never have hatred toward anybody. Yet, at the same time, one should not have any love for that Nation and its government that have invaded one's own Nation.
47. Management sees the business world in black and white, for they are out of touch with the actions of their employees. The employees see their job in color because they are not hidden somewhere in the front office.
48. A Man/s character will speak for him, even when he is unable to speak for himself.
49. We should be more concerned with the way we conduct ourselves, not only when we are in the presence of Mankind. But more so when we are in the presence of God, especially when others are not around.
50. Ignorance is the downfall of a free people and their Nation.

51. Never trust your National government, especially when they have control over your Nation's history.

52. Christ Jesus: The son of God and the son of Man. As we, Mankind, were made in his image and are perfect in his sight, it would only be natural for every race to imagine this Lord God of ours to be in their image because we see ourselves through him who dwells within our spirit. Yet, in truth, when Jesus walked in the flesh, he was of the Hebrew race and was not of mixed blood. We see ourselves as being perfect in him and through him; and therefore we see ourselves as being the same in image as him of race. That is why we have many different images of Christ, for he is the Saviour of all Mankind.

53. No King but King Jesus!

54. We have two kinds of thieves in this world: those that steal from us legally and those who don't steal from us legally.

55. Mankind was created to worship their creator. If they should refuse to worship their true God, then they shall truly worship other false gods.

56. To put a monument of Abraham Lincoln in Richmond, Virginia, is as equally bad and as equally the same as putting a monument of Adolph Hitler in Israel.

57. Mr. Abraham Lincoln is one of many anti-Christs; and his Gettysburg Address is a smoke screen just as it is, without a real foundation of truth.

58. The correct term for the zip code in the Confederacy is: The Yankee occupation code.

59. A true Nation is a Nation that is sovereign; and a true Nation is a Nation that is not ruling over other Nations. A true Nation is a Nation that sets the example of freedom and sovereignty for the whole world to look upon. To force freedom upon other Nations causes the value of that liberty to become cheap and meaningless. Therefore liberty must be from the free will of that Nation's people, and it must be their blood that they are willing to spill in order to obtain that rare jewel of understanding.

60. A spark in the night and a blink of an eye show the value of how precious life was meant to be. If we were to live forever within this flesh of ours, we would no more value life now than we did in the past by all of the death that has been done by the hands of Mankind. To believe in reincarnation is almost the same as wanting immortality of the flesh. If we do not learn from our own mistakes now, in our present lives, then we never will.

61. A world super power or Empire becomes a government full of dictators on a broad scale.

62. Only an idiot would have the audacity to mock the Biblical moral wisdom for Mankind.

63. One of the major problems of being a world super power is the realization that in any direction you turn you will find a Nation that has become your enemy. They will circle you and wait for the right time for you to grow tired and watch for you to drop your guard. They will allow your mistakes to cause you to become like a drunk, who is begging for a thief to rob and kill him.

64. It would have been far better if we (*The Confederate States of America*) were presently under the rulership of Great Britain instead of the United State. The yoke of tyranny would have been less burdensome, and the illusion of our own present liberty would have been less dramatic.

65. Jesus Christ: The name of true salvation and eternal life. It is clear that we, the children of Christ, have forgotten a very simple lesson of our Messiah's paying the price for us. When

Jesus paid the price for our sins, He could only do so by paying the full price that we as sinners would have paid. Even if He had not gone to hell to take back those keys of life and death, He would still have been required to be cast into hell for our sins. Once He had done this, then all of our sins from past to present, including our future sins, were cast into hell with Him. As He has paid our debt for our sinful actions, we have become pure in the eyes of God by His blood. His blood became the down payment for us; and the Holy Ghost became our birthmark, as a family. Therefore, all of our sins are in hell and have been parted from us in true repentance.

66. It is written that we should not become of this world, a world of sin and insanity, a world of foolish ideology and all of the things that are not in the character of Christ and of our Father. The sad truth is that this world has had a strong influence upon our brothers and sisters in Christ. Christians have apologized for their defense of slavery as it is written in the Bible. Christians have become fearful of acting as Christians in public, because they don't want to offend anyone. Some have given support to the idea of homosexuality as not being a sin but a make up of our DNA.

67. Most have also accepted the ideas of miscegenation as well. So it would seem that we have allowed not only a federal government to tell us what we should believe, but we are allowing the whole world to do the thinking for us as well.

68. The treasures of our beloved Confederacy are the people themselves: the different race of each southerner who has made a contribution to our society and those things that make us a people of Confederate Americans. It is natural and normal for every race to want to promote and to preserve their own race. It is also a natural thing for each race to expect themselves to improve and to do better in every way so that they will continue to grow as individuals and as a people of race. It shall also be beneficial to every other Confederate of race; but to allow one race of people to do this and to deny other races this free will is not only the basis of discrimination, it is also an act of denying their rights as citizens of our beloved States in our Confederacy. It is not important to measure the contributions one race may give to our society, for the amount of accomplishments do not make one race supreme over another. Nor does it give them the authority to rule over other races that have contributed far less. It is taking the best from each Confederate, regardless of race, and making it a part of our daily lives as a state and as a Nation, that is important. For if we cannot learn from our Confederate neighbors of different races, and if we cannot learn from ourselves, then what hope do we have to sustain us as a society?

69. "Just because we can, does this mean that we should?"

70. It is apparent that the ability of most people in North America have been affected by idiocy and they are unable to think for themselves. This condition has spread as fast as a forest fire and is as sickening as a stomach virus. It has become as dangerous as the black plague.

71. In war the victory of your Nation and the protection of those under your command come first and above your own honor and fame. To do otherwise would place you in the category of a tyrant.

72. Any military that preys upon the citizens of the Nation in which they are, and brings harm to them, has become a Nation of barbarians and deserves neither mercy, honor, nor safe passage home.

73. Any Nation that wins a war will most likely not pay for any war crimes that they may have committed during that time.
74. To control the minds and hearts of all those who are under your rule becomes the first step in building a world Empire.
75. It should not come to anyone's surprise that those of us who know our true history feel resentful toward those Yankees for: the unconstitutional invasion into our Nation and the aggression toward the sovereignty of our State governments; for the rape, murder, and pillage of our civilians' property and land; for destroying our Republican form of federal government, including the starvation of our people in their war camps and from their coastal blockade; and the intense effort to commit genocide toward our people. The racial strife that they have caused us just because we chose liberty over democracy results in the natural animosity of our Confederate people toward those people and their Nation's Reich. Until we have peacefully regained that which they have stolen from us, we should remember that not every Yankee is an obnoxious, selfrighteous, delusional, idiot. Some of them are a very kind and caring people, who love their family and God, who hold dear the constitutional Republic they had. From them, we ask for understanding and for forgiveness if we have been disrespectful toward them.
76. To live in ignorance is to deny and to reject the justice that is due to those that don't know any better.
77. If justice and safety are not given to those who cannot speak for themselves, (THE UNBORN), then justice and safety cannot be guaranteed to those who can speak for themselves, (THE BORN).
78. A Christian Nation is not only a society that is obedient to the Gospel of Christ, but that State's and federal governments are also under the obedience of our *King Christ* especially more so.
79. Before your death, most people have never heard of you. After your death the media may make a martyr out of you.
80. It is our duty as Christians and as human beings to do our best and to live our lives according to the Gospel of Jesus Christ, to put Him first and then our families, then our friends, and finally, our country. Our duty to everything and everyone else shall only last a short time in our lives; but our duty to Christ Jesus is a lifetime into our after lifetime in living our lives according to His will and the will of His Father. We must know and understand when it is time to let go of certain duties and not allow them to interfere with our other duties and responsibilities. And in all of our duties and responsibilities, we must take Christ with us wherever we go and in everything we do, during our daily lives. We must not try to hid anything from Him nor try and fix our problems without Him. Instead, we must allow Him to be involved in all that we do and allow Him to guide us along this journey of life. We do not nor are we required to walk alone and without hope. He will be with us and within us, and He shall go with us where no one else can go.
81. It may be a question to others whether or not there is a Jesus Christ and why He hasn't returned yet and taken these Christians home with Him. It has been over two thousand years already! My answer to this question would be: The love of the Father is without boundaries and without restraints. The love for His children is without a time frame. He sent His son, on His behalf, to

become the lighthouse within the darkness of this world. Therefore, the gospel of Christ will reach out to all of those from the past, present, and future, so that they may come together in the point of time and be gathered up to be taken to the Father. All of His children have not been accounted for yet. Those children of His in the future must be born in the flesh before they are reborn in the spirit of Christ; and they have a place to make in history just as those before and after us. The simple answer is this: It takes time for Him to gather up all of His children before the end of days.

82. The North American war is very dear and special to our southern or Confederate people. Even though it was not a colonial war, it was still a war to preserve our own independence. The Federalist barbaric actions of tyranny and violations of their own federal constitution caused our Confederate people to stand in defense to preserve our Christian society and home and to fight the foreign infidels that were determined to enslave us under a new revolutionary form of government. It became just as much a Holy war as it was a war of patriotism and survival. The colonial war had become the first phase of our Republican liberty, and the Yankeenite war became the final phase that dismantled it.

83. If this world is unable to appreciate us while we are among the living, then we do not need their appreciation long after we are among the dead.

84. We were created to love and worship and to forever praise our creator to, in the end, become perfect in spirit through the molding of perfection in Christ himself.

85. Let us not walk in the paths of the foolish ones. Let us not embrace the ignorance of those who are lost. And let us not put our hopes in those whose minds are as dull as much as their eyes are blinded from the truth. Let not our ears be filled with their pollution and meaninglessness of words. And let us not believe that we are masters of our own salvation and destiny.

86. It is healthy and normal for us to desire to learn and to understand the different cultures and the philosophies of different peoples and of Nations; but we must not allow it to the point of having such a strong influence that it endangers our own culture and identity, nor to the point that we are required to sacrifice our own culture and our foundation of liberty that as a people became into being. Even learning and understanding have their limitations of danger.

87. This world is influenced and guided by the limitations of rational thought and the emotional feelings of what may be right and wrong. Both bring madness and are suicidal for all of mankind; but in the wisdom of God, through His son, all that was dark becomes light and all that was hidden is now understood. In the spirit, soul, and body, it all comes to one understanding; and that is to understand through the heart and eyes and the words that He brings forth. He is the Alpha and the Omega.

88. If someone comes up and says that any symbols of our Confederate States are symbols of racism and of pro slavery, it can only be for one of three reasons. The first may be of ignorance; the second would be of hatred; and the last, but not least, would be the final outcome of propaganda teachings in public education.

89. I believe the president of the United State of America must be required to apologize to the States of the Union for the violations of the constitutional rights of those State citizens of the Union during the time of the unconstitutional invasion into the Confederate Nation. I believe

that the president of the United State of America must be required to apologize to the States of the Confederacy for that act of aggression and suppression and enslavement of the Confederacy by the chains of Union Rule, including the approval of war crimes by the Union government and president. The sovereignty of the States of the Confederacy and the constitutional federal government of the Confederate States of America must be recognized and stated in public and directed to the media of the entire world. Retributions must be made to the states of the Confederacy of what it cost for the federal and state governments to defend themselves and their sovereign rights, including what it would cost for the rebuilding and overcoming the horrors of that war.

90. Within the righteousness in Christ is the source of purity of heart and forgiveness of the weakness of one's soul. Humbleness and kindness without his righteousness causes weakness in the foundation one's own character, causing it to become brittle and fragile.

91. When a Nation comes to occupy another Nation after a war that occupied Nation's existence falls prey to that foreign aggressor and enslaved. The Culture and language and the ways of thoughts about life and government also fall victim to the master. The whole concept of who and what that fallen Nation is falls on the mercy of its aggressor.

92. How blinded we are at time to believe that our views reign supreme over the liberties that God has given mankind, to believe that other Nations must have the same form of government and religion as ours, to believe that we are superior to others and that everyone must reform themselves to fit into our image and likeness. If we have something that would be a great benefit to this world, then let us freely share our ideas of a constitutional Republic government; and let us share our faith in the Gospel of Christ Jesus. But let us not force our will and ideas against anyone that may reject them, for it is their freedom to choose that we must come to respect and embrace. This does not, however, allow nor justify the rights to violate and to enforce the cruelty of the violation in Human rights. If anyone dares to force themselves upon us, then let us stand in defense and crush anyone that dares to trample upon our God-given liberties.

93. A Nation that is without sin is a Nation without a government. A Nation without sin is a Nation without a National flag. A Nation that is without sin is a Nation without a people. And a Nation that is without sin is a Nation that is not of this Earth.

94. This world is unable to speak with authority as to what the definition of moral sins may be, for it is this world that is living in sin and therefore has no authority to judge itself. According to the Holy Book, sin is a stumbling block toward perfection and salvation; and if it ain't a sin according to the Holy Book, then it's not a sin.

95. If you don't speak with the same accent and write as it has been written and spoken in the King James Bible then you don't speak and write with the proper English language. Therefore, what gives anyone that right to condemn different people that may not speak as they do or who have a different form of accent? And by what right does anyone discriminate against anyone over a job position just by the way they speak the English language or by their accents? The truth is that no one has that right! This is just another form of culture cleansing and discrimination.

96. It was not the requirement for our Confederate Nation to win the war, in order to become free, for it was not us who invaded their Union States. But since they invaded us, we were required

to win the war in order to remain free. As long as we stood up to the aggression of the United States in battle we remained a free people and Nation.

97. The foundation of liberty becomes the platform where a people can build their dreams without someone trampling upon their children's future. And the foundation of liberty must be able to grow and blossom without losing its form or being transformed into something that is not of its true self.

98. The Confederate working class has been transformed into industrial slavery. At times they are required to work more than fortyeight hours and up to seven days a week; and it is required to do the jobs of two or three persons without extra pay. The Yankees have set the Southern governments up in such a way that our people can be used for cheap laborers with fewer restrictions on foreign Yankee companies. The way that the economy is set up, it becomes a no win situation. One or two parents have to work one or two jobs each just to get by. They are not spending enough time at home to enable them to raise their children; and the children are being raised in public schools. The parents don't have enough time for their spouse, let alone time for themselves. And all the while the inflation and unconstitutional taxes keep going up. Each year it becomes harder to make ends meet. Prices go up on all of the products while the quality stays more or less the same; and so you end up paying more for less.

99. In our present day, it is good to be anti-Confederate and to be offended by and condemn any symbols of the Confederacy. For one thing, it would be politically correct; and for the other, it is the way that the United States have rewritten history (in other words, to be anti-Southern). It is my personal view that most people would prefer to submit to the social reengineering and not to offend anyone than to stand up for the truth and act as if they had any backbones. They are afraid of losing their jobs and all of their material objects. They are afraid of harm that would be directed toward their family and their own personal lives. They are afraid of being persecuted and maybe being put in jail. They may even be afraid of learning the truthful history and finding out that they have been living a lie for all of these years. They are not only afraid of the truth but also of having the responsibilities that come along with it. They are not willing to sacrifice even half of what our Confederate and Founding forefathers have sacrificed on our behalf. What will our future generation have to say about us? I wonder!

100. They say that Abraham Lincoln was a Christian before he had taken his last breath. I hope, for his sake, that this is true; but the way that those people are always rewriting their U.S. history, we may never truly know. If anyone were to say that he was a Christian up to the time of his death, then I can only call it as I see it; and that, my friends, would be as an outright lie. Every man has a legacy, and every legacy will lead you to the truth of that man. When if, in the course of his life, he were to change, then that pathway that he had walked should still show traces of his footsteps. With the help of others he crushed the Union of the Republican States. He has portrayed his oath to protect and to sustain the Constitution of those United States of America. He had used the army of the United States to agitate a Christian Nation (*The Confederate States*) to act with aggression in defense of their liberties. He defended the cause of the actions of a Confederate Holocaust in the name of the Union and tariffs. He is guilty of the murders

101. of Confederate POWs in his Union prison camps, as it was clear that the civilians of the Union States and his Federalist troops did not do without proper clothing and food, including medicines. And for the best for last, he was a racist and a supporter of white supremacy over the North American Negroes. And by the way, white supremacy is just as bad as black supremacy. My statement is this: the true history of Lincoln has been whitewashed for the justification of their war toward us.

102. What is the modern man made religion that would be the very replication of the problems that Christ had with the Pharisees and the Sadducees in the New Testament? That religion is *Catholicism*. Just as the Pharisees and the Sadducees had done with the Mosaic Laws, by adding man made laws and rituals, so have the Catholics done to the Gospel of Christ. In truth, the Catholicism is not the true gospel in its pure form. It resembles more a wolf in sheep's clothing than a stairway to Heaven.

Confederate Citizens' Peaceful Protest

1. Always fly your Third National Confederate States Flag.
2. If you don't have a Third National Flag at this time, then fly "The Stars and Bars" or "The Stainless Banner" or "The Bonnie Blue" until you're able to buy The Third National.
3. If you don't have any of the above, then buy a foreign U.S. flag and fly it upside down. This is a sign of S.O.S.; and it denounces the unconstitutional occupation of our Confederate Nation.
4. If you're able, never buy an automobile from any car lot that flies that foreign U.S. flag.
5. If you buy the U.S. postage stamps, put the flag stamp upside down on your envelopes.
6. Whenever you write the address on your mail, if it is a Confederate State, then write that state's name followed by "C.S.A.". If that state is in the union, then write that state's name followed by "U.S.A.".
7. When it's time to cash your pay check, tell that person that you prefer not to have any five dollar bills. Ask for five ones instead.
8. Depending on your situation, if you have any papers that ask if you are a U.S. citizen, answer that you are a citizen of your Southern State.
9. When someone says something about the American Flag, ask them "which flag? The Confederate States' Flag or the U.S. flag, or the flag of Mexico or what?"
10. When you go into a place of business or someone's house and you see a picture of Abraham Lincoln, ask them if they knew that one of Lincoln's favorite admirers was Adolf Hitler, and tell them that he used some of Lincoln's tactics during World War II.
11. Confederate citizens should always pay their extortion fees (income taxes) to the United States government, until we've regained our national independence once more.
12. Always give your highest compliments to all individuals who display our Confederate emblems and Southern products in public places.
13. When you're able, never buy any products from anyone that flies any foreign U.S. or other foreign flags.
14. Time to purchase a produce! Buy C.S. products of the Southern States first! Then overseas products. Next, and if necessary, buy
15. U.S. products.
16. Never ever buy any U.S. bonds!
17. Confederate citizens should never stand up and take the oath or sing any foreign national anthem that is not of The Confederate States of America.

18. Never pledge allegiance to anyone or any thing that is not The Lord and King Jesus Christ.
19. Boycott any organizations and industries that are anti-Southern, anti-Christian, and anti-Constitutional of the Republic.
20. Never sell out your people and your Confederate Nation by selling your land to any foreign industries or organizations. Wealth cannot buy the freedom that your future grandchildren were meant to have in the first place!
21. If you're able, put your children in a private or home school. Reeducate yourself and your children about the history and culture of your people; and learn the true meaning of God and country.
22. If your children must serve in the foreign forces of the United States, make them understand why they should not take the oath and serve under the command of the United Nations under any condition.

I WOULD LIKE TO THANK DR. MICHAEL HILL, PRESIDENT OF THE LEAGUE OF THE SOUTH, FOR HIS GUIDANCE AS I STARTED TO WRITE THE CONFEDERATE CITIZENS' PEACEFUL PROTEST

In Recognition Of
The Confederate States Of America

To the leaders and citizens of every Nation of this Earth: I request your attention to the statement that I am about to make on behalf of my subjected people and of an occupied Nation. Every person is welcome to study our history and to learn of our truthful past, and though it is not required for other Nations to recognize publicly the existence of these Confederate States of America, it would, none the less, be welcome.

1. That by the understanding our Confederate forefathers of the United States Declaration of Independence, including the federal Constitution of the United States of America, that they acted within the right to withdraw and to defend the sovereignty of their State governments.
2. That the Sovereignty of the States governments is within their boundaries In creating the federal government of these Confederate States.
3. That the Confederate States government establishes that **God** Himself is in control of this Nation.
4. That the blood and the deaths of our comrades in arms have defended in defense of our States Constitutions and the federal Constitution of our Confederate States of America.
5. The Confederate government has established peace treaties with the Native American Indians and has sent diplomats on behalf of the Confederate government to other Nations.
6. That the Southern States had established the federal constitution of these Confederate States of America.
7. That the Confederate States tried to establish a peace treaty with the United States, but were treated disrespectfully by the refusal of the United States to speak with our diplomats.
8. That the Confederate States had a federal reserve.
9. That the Confederate States had a National flag.
10. That the Confederate States had a National Seal, known as *The Great Seal*.
11. That the Confederate States had a monetary system.
12. That the Confederate States had a Navy and State Militia.
13. That the Confederate States had a trade system with other countries.
14. That the Confederate States government has never signed a treaty of surrender of any kind to the United States.

The Confederate States of America has earned the right in so many ways to be recognized as a sovereign Nation, according to its own federal constitution. Be that our Nation has been baptized by the blood of liberty in battle. And that being that we were the victims that fought to the best of our abilities against the aggressions of our foe. We can only hope that *Christ our King* will recognize the rights of our Confederacy. And that history shall stand in our defense to the Nations of this world. Thank you.

Yours truly, John Thomas Nall

Patriotism

We embrace the ideas of our Founding Fathers and their true American Republic. So, we fought to preserve it.

We believe in the Declaration of Independence and acted upon it. We loved the U.S. Constitution and improved it for our nation.

Feeling the inner duty of patriotism as our Founding Fathers before us, we established our final "3rd National Flag"; and we established our National Song: "God Save The South".

We created a small nation and at the same time we defended her against the most powerful nation of the world. We were born out of blood and tears, prayers, and the principles of our ancestors. In God and Country, our National Flag is without blemish.

"The Confederate States of America"

20 April 1997

Our Country's Flag

I am The Third National, the flag of my country, and I am here before you to state my case, so that you may know the meaning of who I am.

What do I stand for? I stand for many things. I am the identity of the life of the Southern People. I am a reminder to them and to the rest of the world, that the Southern People are also in truth "Confederates".

I am a symbol of a Christian nation, because I am the rebirth of The Scotland Flag of Saint Andrews Cross. Many Christian Confederates fought and also died to keep me and my staff from lying on the ground during battle.

I am resistance to the philosophy and the system of communism and of democracy, because I am a symbol of the free will of the people within the states in which they live, of a constitutional form of the government of the republic.

I am a symbol of my country, for it was the Declaration of Independence that became the reason for my being. I am also a reminder of the blood of liberty from the veins of our Southern Brothers, who made a stand in our defense, that watered our land.

I am a reminder of the self-determination of self-preservation of that Godgiven right of liberty, for no man and no other nation has the right to take it away from our people.

I represent, forever and always, every Southerner of every race who has fought for me and who is a Southerner by birth, as this is their land.

I am a symbol of the culture and heritage, and the English language with a Southern flavor, of a Christian society.

I stand for that which is the truth, that shall not perish, for it is our Heavenly Father Who shall right the wrong in our defense.

I am many things, and yet I am only one. So, therefore, I do not have to question why there are those who feel the need to hate me!

18 JANUARY, 2000

Strangers In Our Own Land

Here we are, living within the great states of the Confederacy; and yet, when we display our Southern colors, we begin to be knocked down by the eyebrows of the Socialist left. I find it wrong, in every aspect of my thinking, that we as a Southern people and our Southern neighbors of other races are discriminated against in every way, when we promote our Southern Heritage within our Southern borders. And yet, when I turn around, I may see those foreign occupational flags ("Yankee flags"). No matter where I'm driving to or coming from, they are everywhere. However, what I would hope to see someday soon is our 3rd National Flag of the Confederate States being flown instead. I personally do not care if I offend others outside of our Southern borders. If they don't like our flags, or the way that we talk, or our way of living, or even our flags, then it's best that they stay where they are because they aren't welcome around here. If they hate our Confederate Flags because of the issue of slavery, that goes to show how ignorant they are on this subject. However, to attack our flag is also a direct attack upon our people and myself; and that's when we take it personally. Those Yankee flags offend me every morning when I'm going to work. It's no different than having the U.S. Flag or any other foreign flag on Southern soil. If the United States had lost the war with Japan (World War II), then they would understand our point of view. Everywhere you looked, you would find that flag of The Rising Sun being flown on Union soil because the United States would be part of the Japanese Empire.

We do not always fly our flags, just for the celebration of our heritage and for our culture. We also fly them for patriotic reasons. We do, however, find that those who would display our colors for the reasons of racial pride end up becoming overwhelmed with ignorance and stupidity. Every Southerner or every race fought and died to defend these flags, our homes, and our families, regardless of whether they worn the gray or were citizens. Personal problems, etc. were put to the side in order to stand side by side to push those Yankee invaders back outside of our Confederate borders.

The war did not take place in some faraway land that you would only hear about in the news. The war took place in our next-door neighbor's backyards. Our citizens suffered the same fate or results as did our Confederate forces. We suffered the same tragedy that was bound to take place in countries of Europe during World War I and II. And if we, "The Confederate People", should ever forget how close our people came to being exterminated, this would make room for history to repeat itself. Was it not Southerners who fought with the Yankees against the Nazis? How dare anyone compare our Christian flag to the Nazi flag! Whosoever is found to be using any flags of the Confederacy for racial purposes should be fined and made to serve time in jail, because that is not a validation of free speech. Using flags in that way is bringing dishonor upon our Confederate dead. These Celtic flags no longer belong to just the white race, but to ever Southerner of every race. Remember, this was not a race war. This was a war between two countries: The United States and the Confederate States. These flags represent the Gospel of Christ; and they are, in truth, "Christian flags", and they deserve the respect that goes along with it.

It is up to us Southerners to protect our symbols of honor from abuse by those who use them in dishonorable ways and to stand guard against those who attack us, because of their ignorance and hatred toward our symbols and ourselves. The U.S. continues to rewrite history in order to justify their actions of victory over us and the war crimes their ancestors had committed against our ancestors. Their reply to this would be that "That was war!"

And now we have corporations and industries boycotting the state of South Carolina because the state government and most of the citizens of that state had no desire to remove the Confederate Navy Jack or Battle Flag from the top of their state capitol. The word "boycott" is a nice way of saying "blackmail". Some of these businesses are originally from our states of the Confederacy; but they don't mind the discrimination against our Southern people nor the taking of Yankee money. It is true that some of these businesses are doing this because they fear any organization that has the federal government as their bodyguard. The rest of these corporations are doing this for other reasons. It's called "politically profitable". For example, they say they are against our Confederate flags because of the subject of slavery; and yet they don't mind supporting the Communist country of China. Don't get me wrong, I love the Chinese people. Their government, however, is an evil institution, a Communist government that is a threat to every country in the world. And here they are, selling products over here that were made in China. It could just be that they may have factories over there as well. As long as they support the economy of China by doing so, the Communist form of government will continually sustain itself. Human rights valuations and slave labor will not improve.

The fact is that they do not care about the truth or true history. They do not care about freedom or human rights. They do not care what color you are, because the only color that they care about is the color of the paper that is in your wallet or purse. When someone has a sweat shop up North, you don't hear much of an out cry from the Northern public.

It has come to the point that almost every form of business is, in one way or another, discriminating against our Southern people; and I'm talking about all Southerners of every race, including the discrimination against our accent within the media business. Don't you ever get tired of having to listen to someone on your local news who sounds like they came from California? Are you not tired of the same ole lies of having them say it's bad for business to speak Southern? The real reason they don't like it is because they are ashamed of having you around or they don't like you because you are not the same as they are. Don't you ever get tired of having them tell you what you should think; how you should feel; what you should believe; what to buy; what you should eat; and who you are?

We are being treated like foreigners in our own land, as if our ancestors and our history aren't about us or about the land in which we live but about some evil country in a faraway land that the United States had to make war on in order to save the world from being themselves.

God's Own Country

It was said that it was the will of God for the Confederate States to lose the war. It was said that the United States was to be the right hand of God in order to destroy the evil slave states of the Confederacy. Both of these are false statements. We do know that the statement about slavery being a sin is not even written within the Holy Bible. We also understand that people, who are in this world, will ignore the Bible and decide for themselves what is right and wrong in their own eyes. Some people would like to believe that it was God who wanted to choose the United States to become the chosen people to right the wrongs in this world. However, this is not true either. If God wanted to punish the Confederate States of America because of slavery he would also have to punish every Nation on Earth, including the United States of America. I should also point out that God doesn't need the United States to do His work, for He is able to do it Himself. I should also point out that it is the Hebrew people of Israel who are His chosen ones and not the United States of America. Moreover, we do not live under the Old Testament laws. The actions of the United States toward the Confederate States would definitely not show the actions of our Christ Jesus. To use the name of God in order to justify the actions of war could only be classified as blasphemy because it goes against the teachings of our Lord Jesus Christ.

When the United States was marching upon the Confederate States and singing the Battle Hymn of the Republic, they should have remembered this, from the Holy Bible: Every Nation is responsible to answer to God for the sins they have committed. They must go and ask for forgiveness and turn away from their sins. Who are they to judge and punish other Nations for the sins or actions that they look on with disapproval? Christ Jesus is the king of all of the Nations of the Earth, including the Confederate States of America. It is Jesus Christ who shall judge the Confederate States, for her sins. And no one else! Every Nation has fallen short in the presence of our Lord God, for no one is without sin. Therefore, no one has the right to cast the first stone and to spill the blood of another sinner. It is written in Psalm 117: *Praise the Lord, all you nations; extol Him, all you peoples. For great is His love toward us, and the faithfulness of the Lord endures forever. Praise the Lord.* Let every Nation, great and small, powerful and fragile, always hold this verse close to their hearts. Here is something that you might find interesting. It comes from the first paragraph of the constitution of the Confederate States of America.

> *We, the people of the Confederate States, each state acting in its sovereign and independent character, in order to form a permanent federal government, establish justice, ensure domestic tranquility, and secure the blessings of liberty to ourselves and our posterity – invoking the favor and guidance of Almighty God – do ordain and establish this Constitution for the Confederate States of America.*

You will not find anything like this written in the constitution of the United States. I should also say that it is not the Confederate States that are forcing abortion clinics and the teaching of the evolution of humanity to our children. However, because of these influences, our Confederate people are also taking part in these sins, and in other sins as well. Christ Jesus appointed his disciples to go out and to share the good news. It was not his desire to force the good news on anybody. It was a gift, from his Father. It was free to everyone because it was Christ who paid the cost for that gift. He has given everyone the free will to accept this gift or to reject it. It is not written anywhere in the Holy Bible that any nation should ever be appointed to force another form of government upon another nation, nor to force its customs upon another. This is not the will of God. In addition, this is not the role that a Christian nation should take part in. The only thing that would please our Heavenly Father would be for the nations to reach out and to give humanitarian aid to those nations who are in need. Nevertheless, it would not be a blessing for any nation to do this and expect something in return. Human lives and the suffering of others should never be used as a bargaining chip to benefit one's wealth or power. If a nation had the desire to set up a fund to buy Bibles, etc., as well as to help train the Christian missionaries, that would be the way to go. This is my point of view.

The gospel of Christ can reach out and heal the nations of the earth. The Holy Bible is like a medicine bag that is filled with the directions for the medicines inside it. However, it must be used correctly. It was meant for the United States of America and the Confederate States of America to be founded on a Christian foundation, for both states' and federal governments, including the Christian society that we once had. That duty falls on us all. I would like to cover some other things: *The day of thanks.* The day of Thanksgiving is a special holiday to both our nations. It is a day to remember our Heavenly Father's gift, for He had brought some of his flocks to the North American shore in order to protect them from the persecution of Catholicism. At that time, the Catholic had established itself as an empire over Europe. If you did not accept the Catholic faith, you would be persecuted or put to death. Some people believe that the Catholic faith and the Christian faith are the same; but the truth is that they are not. The Catholic church is another form of a denominational church. Once the Pilgrims had made it to North America, they established a good and a close relationship with one of the North American Indian tribes. In fact, if it had not been for the Indians' guidance throughout the season, the Pilgrims would have died from the cruelty of nature. The reason the Indians had established a relationship with the Pilgrims was not because they were a white race. Nor was it for their technology or the fact that they approved of the invasion by these Pilgrims. It was because these Pilgrims were a Christian people.

The Pilgrims were trying to live by the teachings and principles of the New Testament. They had no desire to take more land than they needed; and they could be a people who seemed to be trust worthy. These Pilgrims also had a respect for the way of life of these different people in this new land. The problem was the heathens from Europe, who were flooding this new land and taking more land than they needed, with no respect for the Indian tribes that lived here. This is the reason that the division between the Pilgrims and the Indians had begun. Before that, they were trading and sharing different ideas with each other. This may have been one of the biggest tragedies that could have taken place. This would have been a perfect time to share and establish a missionary outreach with their Indian friends. Unfortunately the people from Europe had other ideas on their mind.

Indeed, we should give thanks to our Lord for our homes, our countries, for those who are indeed our true friends, and most of all for Christ. This is where the subject about the separation of church and states comes in. The separation of church and state was designed to keep any religious organizations and establishments from having control over the federal government, in order to protect the Christian people and others of different religions. It was to deter the use of the federal government as a tool of persecution. However, the foundation of the federal government was established on the philosophy of Christianity. This was established by our Founding Fathers. I reassure you that anyone who is a Christian, or from any other religion, or even an atheist, can hold office in the federal government so long as they do not undermine the Christian principles on which the federal government was established. To do so would still be an act of treason.

The other thing I would like to share with you is this: It was not the will of God to deny the rights of the southern people to their own and separate country. It is more important to Our Heavenly Father to watch over the conduct of his children. Christianity did drift from place to place in the old South; however, it did not take hold of our people, as a nation, until after the war was in progress. It showed in the tent revivals that were spreading through the lines of the Confederate States' forces. Every moment that ticked by, some Confederate was out there in the field, longing to go home, but knowing that he must go forth when it was necessary to defend his family, home, and country. The thought of dying was always in the back of his mind. I am sure that thought has gone through the minds of the invading soldiers of the United States as well. The Confederate military were always outnumbered, yet they continually won battles over the tyrant foes. I do believe it was our Lord God who was, at that time, with the men of Grey. The sad thing was that we did not give all the glory to our God.

The Confederate soldiers were giving all the glory to themselves. After some time, God withdrew his hand and allowed the Confederate people to fall into the hands of their foreign oppressors. It is a hard lesson that the world is still trying to learn to this day. God does not care about the country that we are from. He does care about our hearts and what is within each of us. If our Confederate ancestors had not made such a big mistake during that time, we would not be still living under that same oppression to this day. All that we are doing at the moment is living off the rotten fruit that is from that tree of tyranny. Indeed God is punishing us, not for such foolishness as slavery, but for not giving all that we have and all that we are to Him. We need to give Him all the glory and hold nothing back. It is one thing to have your own country. It is another to earn it and keep it by the grace of our Lord God. Our Lord God did not deny the people the right to form a new country of their own (The United States of America). Therefore He would not deny our people that same right, to protect and defend those rights that He has given humankind under a different banner than our own. There are different countries everywhere on this earth. Not all of them are Christian nations. So how could you say it was His will to deny the southern states their own country and yet allow those who rejected his Son to have their own? I should also remind you that most of these countries are still practicing slavery at this very moment.

The truth is that you cannot truly understand the physical part of liberty without first understanding the spiritual part. What good is your physical freedom if your spiritual salvation is lost forever? Indeed the Confederate States has earned the right to be free, for we are, in truth, a separate country. But until we, as a Confederate people, learn that it is the spiritual freedom that is the very framework for the physical freedom that our founding and Confederate forefathers were willing to fight and die for, we will not be able to make much of a difference to the rest of this world. Freedom is not some kind of mystical ideology from someone's imagination. It is the reality of being able to walk with our heads held high and to act according to the intentions that our God had for us, not to yield to Satan and to those that are being influenced by him. This world has two kinds of role models for humankind to live their lives by. The first one is Jesus Christ. The second one is Satan. Whenever a person or a government desires to dominate the world and to build an empire on the bones of any free people, anywhere or at any time, then, in truth, this is close to repeating the role that Satan played against God. Satan wants to rule over Heaven and earth and to take the throne away from God. Since we are made in the image of our creator, then Satan would most likely want to destroy us all as well. For we would always be a reminder to Satan of who the real creator is. God has given his Son a free will. He has given his angels a free will. He has also given us a free will. Nevertheless, when someone or some country desires to rule over another country, then they are denying the people from that other country the right to have a free will. They desire to do the very same thing that Satan wants to do, for these are the same actions, whether by Satan or humankind, that show the desire to override and to take away the authority that our God has established for all of his creation.

I am asking all Christians to pray this prayer with me. If you believe in fasting, then I also am asking you to fast, for as many days as you feel led to do so.

> *Our Heavenly Father:*
>
> *Each one of your children who are living in North America and who are praying this prayer ask that you will listen to our prayers. We are asking you to forgive the United States of America for the war crimes that they have committed toward the Confederate States of America and throughout the world. We ask not for vengeance, our Lord. We ask only that they leave us in peace and, in addition, become our friends for as long as we are both obedient to you. We pray that you will restore the Republican form of government of the United States and their country's states and federal constitutions. We ask that you will watch over and protect all of our brothers and sisters in Christ who live there. We ask that you will guide and protect the people that are striving to restore the foundation of their country and to protect their family members from danger as well.*
>
> *We are asking for your recognition and blessings for the Confederate States of America and that which is written in our state constitutions and the constitution of the Confederate States of America. We ask for the guidance and wisdom for those who are in the service of their leaders in this government; we ask also for those who have been chosen to be leaders for the member states' governments including the federal government of the Confederacy. We pray that their hearts shall always be humble and that they will remember that they are never too far from your eyes, that you hear every whisper beneath their breath. Let us not, as a people and as a country, continually stumble in this darkness with amnesia. Not only are we lost without you, dear Lord, but we have also come to lose the knowledge of our true selves. We ask that you will forgive our people and country of our sins, for we need You to show us the way to become pleasing in your sight. Restore our Confederacy as a Christian society once more, so that we can live in harmony with our southern neighbors of different races. Let us not forget the contributions of every true Confederate, regardless of race, sex, or age, for it was both the slaves and the free who fought and died in defense of our country and in the name of freedom. Let us not forget these things dear Lord. Let us always remember your*

supreme sovereignty over all things and above everyone, for we as a people and as a country shall always be in the service of our Lord and King, Jesus Christ.

Thank you, in Jesus' Name, Amen.

God would bless the Confederate States and the United States in so many ways, if they would broaden their concepts about foreign policy. I tell you the truth, it was the Gospel of Christ what brought down the Berlin wall and crushed the head of Communist Russia. It was not the military might or policies of the United States. The Gospel is able to defeat the evil philosophies that would go against the teachings of Christ Jesus. This can be done, without destroying other countries and their people. Our federal governments should support the Christian missionaries, not control or interfere with them. We cannot force salvation on any one, nor are we able to stop some countries from going to war. However, the gospel can change the hearts and minds of a whole country, thus changing the way of their people, their country's views and reactions toward the other countries all over this world. War has never been able to prove which side was right or justify aggression. War should only be used as a last resort in defiance of an invasion. Peace talks should continue until there is no hope for peace. Before we can ever be able to help other countries of this world, we must first change our ways as Christian nations, in order to set an example to every country looking in our direction. Therefore it should be a policy for the federal governments of the Confederate States and the United States to restructure their ideas on foreign policy.

I understand that some people in this world believe that Jesus was a good teacher, etc., but that He is not the Son of God. They have a right to their opinions, and I respect their decision. Yet they can still take the teachings of Jesus and apply them to their lives. Let me share a different story with you. The title of the story is *Trigger's Downfall*. There was a farmer, and he had a young, healthy dog. He took the time to train and to help the dog understand the importance of the dog's duty. That duty was to watch over and protect the farm at all times. If the danger was too great, the dog's duty was to run to his master and warn him of the danger. After some time, the farmer and the dog became close friends. The farmer decided to give his dog the name of Trigger. Whenever the farmer was out in the fields, Trigger would always be second in command over the livestock. Certain times during the winter, food became scarce; and the predators would have to go out of their way to search for more food. One day a bobcat came down from the cliffs nearby. The bobcat came from behind some small boulders behind the farmer. It was much too far away, and the farmer could not see or hear much from where he was. However Trigger could sense that something was wrong. He also noticed a scent that was not of the herds. As he went to check it out, the bobcat jumped out from behind the rocks and attacked one of the sheep. The bobcat went straight for the throat and killed the sheep. By the time Trigger got there, it was too late. He did jump on the bobcat and fur started to fly everywhere. The farmer heard the sound of fear that was spreading through the herd; and he took his shotgun and headed in that direction. As soon as he got there, he saw the fight that was taking place; but it was much too dangerous for him to use his shotgun because his dog was in the line of fire. So he held his gun up toward the sky and fired a round. That was all it took. The bobcat ran way; and Trigger wasn't hurt too badly, because he had the surprise attack in his favor. Then one night, as everyone was asleep, a badger began sneaking around the barn. Trigger was sleeping in front of the fireplace. As soon as he heard the noise from outside, he held up his head and lifted his ears to listen more carefully. It seems that the badger was trying to get some raw eggs for breakfast before the rooster started to crow, but the chickens were not too happy about the badger's idea.

Once Trigger realized that the sound might be some form of danger, he got up and ran through the pet door out the kitchen door. By the time he got to the barn and saw the badger, the farmer was just getting out of bed and trying to put his pants on in the dark. Trigger went straight for the badger; and suddenly it was a free for all. That badger was just too much for any dog to handle. The farmer came running out of the house and into the doorway of the barn. This is where he found Trigger, lying beside a bale of hay, covered in his own blood. It was too dark to use the shotgun; and he was afraid he might kill some of his livestock in the barn. He knew that the badger might still be somewhere in the barn. Holding a flashlight in his left hand, he took his shotgun and laid it against one of the beams of the barn. Most of his outside tools, like shovels, etc., were right behind the doorway. He reached over behind the doorway and grabbed a pitchfork. Then he took his flashlight and started to shine it in the direction of the right front corner inside the barn. Slowly moving the light from the corner toward the middle, he determined that section of the barn to be clear. Then he began moving it from the middle toward the back right corner of the barn. That section looked clear as well. Starting over again, he moved the light from the back right corner of the barn toward the middle section of the back wall. This area seemed fine also. Again, he shines his light from the middle of the back wall toward the back left corner of the wall. All of a sudden, he saw the badger trying to crawl out between a small crack at the bottom of the wall and the ground. At first the farmer jumped back with fear, then he got hold of himself. The badger could not work his way between the small opening near the bottom of the floor. It seemed that the badger had put himself between a rock and a hard place. The farmer took his pitchfork and pierced the badger, then stabbed the badger again; and you could hear the sound of pain. The badger was fighting for his life; and he attacked the pitchfork. The farmer stabbed the badger again, but this time it went all the way through; and the badger died.

The farmer walked over to check on Trigger, but Trigger was unable to move, although he was holding his own. The farmer knew it is not wise to touch an injured animal, because an injured animal might turn on the owner and bite him, due to fear and pain. So he turned around and headed back into the house, called the veterinarian, and informed him about the situation. While on the phone, he was also trying to explain to his wife what had taken place, as well. The doctor told the farmer to stay with the dog until he could get there. The farmer told the doctor he would do so; and then he hung up the phone and went back to the barn to give the dog some company. The veterinarian finally showed up and gave Trigger a shot for the pain. He had to make about 13 stitched; and he gave the farmer some pills to crush and place in the dog's food. Around six weeks went by and Trigger was becoming his old self. A few years passed after that, and Trigger was growing up to be a real guard dog and protector around the farm. He always tried to watch his master's back. However, one day Trigger was lying on the front porch of the house; and he began to wonder to himself about the farms around his area. It crossed his mind that if he could do such a great job on his own farm, then he might be able to make a difference in other places as well. After some time, he finally convinced himself that this would be a good idea. He got up the next morning and took off on his new adventure. The first place he went was a farm about a half mile down the road. Once he got there, he decided to take a quick look around to see what changes would need to be made before he got started.

Two strange dogs walked up to him and started growling and showing their teeth. It seems that these two dogs lived on the farm, and they were not very happy about Trigger's presence and the way he was taking over their farm. Nevertheless Trigger, in his own mind, believed that his way was best, that if it works great for him and everyone on his farm, then it should also be good for everyone else. Therefore he tried to explain himself to the two dogs. He tried to give his own dog point of view, but when the dogs jumped on him and started to attack him, it was evident that they were not very happy with his ideas. The two dogs ran poor Trigger off their farm. He was more upset and saddened by the situation. It was not so much that his pride was hurt, but that he could not understand why those dogs acted that way toward him. As he was putting this ungrateful farm behind him, he decided to head toward another farm about two miles away, making him about two and a half miles from his own farm. Arriving there, he took a good look over the area. He decided to cut across the field and head toward the back of the house. As he was coming around the back, he saw an old barn in the background. Beside the barn was a fenced in area where the farmer was feeding his chickens. As Trigger approached the fence, the farmer saw a blurred image from the corner of his eye, turned around, and saw the dog on the other side of the fence.

So the man stopped feeding the chickens and stepped outside the fence. He walked over to the dog and was really surprised to see how friendly the dog was. Trigger became very fond of his new friend, who did not have a dog. So Trigger felt that he could hang around this farm for a few days and put things in order. After a couple of days had gone by, Trigger decided to head home. A few hours later, he was going up the dirt road, toward his home farm. He started to sense that something was very bad, but he wasn't sure why. By the time he got to the farm, he noticed that his master's house was burned down, to the ground. He became filled with fear and confusion. Heading toward the house, it appeared that the fire had been out for some time, but it was still smoking. Trigger decided to search through the debris to see if he could find his master. He found the body of a dead human, near the back of the master's bedroom. The body was almost completely burned through and it was as black as charcoal; however there was enough of the unburned flesh around the area of the face to identify the remains.

This was enough for Trigger to know that the body was that of his master's wife. He headed to the back of the house. As he got there, he saw a body lying on the ground, face down. It was near a tractor, which was parked underneath a big, old, oak tree. He slowly walked over to the body with his head hung low. As he got nearer, he surmised that it was a man, but he could not see this human's face because the face was turned in the other direction. He walked slowly around the body and realized that it was his master. Starting to lick his unmoving master's face, he saw a big hole in the middle of his back. Blood was all over the body and the ground. He licked the face once more, but the master's face was very cold. After about twenty minutes, an ambulance, a fire truck, and a police car drove up to the farm. Trigger knew the master was dead, but he wouldn't let anyone else come near the body. One of the police officers decided to call the veterinarian on the car phone and ask him to handle the dog so that they could take care of the body. After the veterinarian drove up, he gave Trigger a shot of tranquilizer. When Trigger finally awoke, he was at the veterinarian's hospital. Trigger was filled with sorrow and grief. He would not eat and he would not sleep, for he had just lost everything that was important to him. He lost his home and human family; and he no longer desired to live without them. He believe that the disaster was his fault. If he had been doing his duty, protecting his farm and all that lived on it, instead of trying to change all that was not in his control, nor his duty, nor his responsibility, then just maybe he could have done something to prevent this disaster.

While Trigger was on his way to change the farms in other areas, two prisoners from Stanton County prison had broken out and were on the run. They hitched a ride on a train, which took them thirty miles from the prison area. They decided it was time to jump off the train and change their transportation, which is how they came across the home of Trigger. While the farmer was in the back, doing his thing, the prisoners broke in the front door and found the farmer's wife inside. They tied her up, found the farmer's shotgun, walked up behind him, and shot him in the back. After killing the farmer, they went back inside the house. They made the farmer's wife cook food for them; and once they were finished eating, they made her go to the back bedroom, where they raped and beat her. After they had their fun, they hit her hard enough to knock her out and set the house on fire. The prisoners believed the fire would keep some of the police busy while they made their getaway. So they found the farmer's old truck and hot wired it. Word has it that in one of the other counties, a truck ran an intersection; and a police car was hiding behind one of those billboards. When the police tried to pull the truck over, someone inside the truck pulled out a shotgun and fired at the police. The police took their car, ran into the truck, and caused it to crash into a tree. One prisoner was killed and the other was taken into custody.

I can share with you two ways that we, as a people, can learn from this story. To a patriotic people, liberty is like a rare jewel that only we, as a people and as a country, own. We cannot give this rare jewel to another people and their country. To do so would be denying our own people access to this and using the jewel in our own way. However, we are able to share information with others all over the world about what this rare jewel looks like and how it has changed and made a difference for our people and country. Once this has been done, it will fall into the hands of all people throughout this world by their going out and digging in their own land. One day they might find another jewel just like the one we have. On the other hand, they may find a very different jewel that is perfect for them. Whatever jewel they find, we should be happy for them, but mind our own affairs. We should always watch over our jewel and protect it from theft by thieves in other countries. Most of all, we should watch over and protect it from our own people with evil hearts of treason, for the value and meaning of this rare jewel would only be held dear to the hearts of those who have earned it – much more than to those to whom it was given and had not earned the right to it. Nor would there be much vale and understanding of it to those that have stolen or destroyed it.

The other way to look at this story would be from a Christian point of view. We believe in sharing the gospel throughout this world. We believe in having a Christian nation. The strange thing is that we also believe that we should not be involved in worldly things. This is one area in which we have allowed Satan to get the best of us. We are supposed to stay away from the sinful things of this world. It was never the will of God to have his children hide in their closets, nor to allow those lost souls, who belong to the prince of darkness, to rule over his children. Truly, these are the reason that there are evil laws approved and passed. Our Christian rights are being violated in this day and time because we have allowed these things to take place. How can we have a Christian nation without having Christian leaders and servants within our state and federal governments? To be honest, we cannot! It is impossible for us to live in a Christian society when we have politicians who go around and play with the emotions of the people, using the words of *God and Country*, as well as the same old smokescreen over the concerns of family values. When have you heard a politician give testimony about finding Christ Jesus? All right then, how about a written testimony from a politician who found the salvation of Christ Jesus? Politicians have learned the old Abraham Lincoln sidesteps. I call it this because the old tyrant Lincoln understood that the best way to get elected was to make all the voters believe that he was one of them. Once in office, you can do everything that you have not been voted in to do. Our Confederate people have two other statements about politicians of this kind. Sometimes we call them turncoats; and at other times, we might say they are riding the fence. All you have to do is look at their political record and compare it to their speeches.

So many times I have heard people making the statement: *I do not care what other people are doing, as long as they do not push it on me!* Everyone has the crazy notion that they live in their own invisible bubble. Moreover, they do not care what is going on in the world or what is having an affect on their neighbors, so long as somebody does not burst their bubble or shake their tree. However, I have news for this kind of people. You cannot stick your head in the sand while leaving the rest of your body exposed for the whole world to attack. As long as you have someone trying to force some sort of social engineering or political changes on your neighboring states, those issues will affect your state as well. You may think that it will never fall into you lap, but do not worry! If you will not yield to their transformation, then they will just have to transform your children and their grandchildren. As long as we are forced to live under a Democracy, all power is taken away from our state governments, as well as the ability they had to protect us and our way of life. Instead of our going through the natural, slow changes of time, changes are being made for us; and we are denied the right to decide what changes we need or want. I ask that everyone consider this carefully! Your life will have an effect on someone else. It might be directly or indirectly. It might be for the best, or it could be for the worst. That depends on you. I can only hope that the noble states of the Confederacy and the noble states of the Union will awaken from the long years of hibernation. May all of the holographic illusions of our false sense of security and liberty vanish away with our ignorance, naive, and awaken dreams.

John T. Nall
13 November 2001

First Of November Of 2001   (Phasing Out)

It is my opinion that it was never the intention of the Federalist or centralized leaders to federalize the member states of the union all at once. I believe that their goal was to slowly wean the member states off of the constitution of the United States. I say this because, if they had enforced the full power of Democracy at one time and removed the constitution from the people, a real civil war or a revolution would have taken place. Directly or indirectly, the Southern states felt that something was not right. They might not have been able to put a finger right on it; however, it was enough to make them question the protection of their state governments. A Republic and a Democracy cannot function together under the same roof within one government. The constitution of the United States is "the letter of the law" or "the law of the land" within the Union borders. Nevertheless, at this time, it is a dead letter because Democracy has replaced the Republic government form and shall slowly regulate the liberties of the people until the people are able to accept the total rule of Democracy. At any time, for any reason, that someone tries to replace the government of the Republic with any other form of government, it is an act of treason toward the people who are state members in the Union, regardless of whether or not it is done from within or from outside of the government. This is still an act of treason. Treason and the death penalty should go together, hand in hand. In fact, I think that there should be an Oak tree planted in front of the White House of the United States and of the Confederate States, which should be used as the hanging tree for politicians who violate their country's constitution, that of the United States and of the Confederate States. This hanging tree should also be used for military members and for those who assassinate any state or government member. The death penalty should also be given to any one who commits treason against their state's constitution. Those committing treason should also receive the death penalty within that state.

It is unconstitutional for the United States government to join any other organizations or partnerships with any other countries which would jeopardize the amount of sovereignty given to the United States government from the constitution of the United States. It is also unconstitutional for the United States government to do this and jeopardize the sovereignty of the state members and their constitutions through a partnership or organization with other countries who may not recognize this sovereignty.

It is also unconstitutional to have the military of the United States serve under a foreign banner. To do so is an act of submission and compromises the sovereignty of the federal government. Since the constitution of the United States of America became the foundation for the constitution of the Confederate States of America, and also since the Confederate States is also a Republican form of government, all the aforementioned applies to the Confederate States government as well. Some people believe that it would be important for the southern states to stay within the Union in order to restore the Republic of the United States.

This would never work out for the best. The southern states are not constitutional members within the Union. The constitution of the United States is not the letter of the law within the Confederate borders. It is not the responsibility of the people of the Confederacy to interfere with the internal affairs of the union. The Southern people are unable to change or make a difference in the pathway that the United States has taken. We were unable to prevent them from invading our country and overthrowing our Confederate states federal government. We are always outvoted in the U.S. congress. Moreover, our people have been brainwashed to the point that they have embraced this false form of government of Democracy. They are taught to be ashamed of their birthright as well as their lifestyle and southern ways. This Yankee Empire of Democracy has been built upon the bones and blood of our Confederate people. As a Confederate people, we should and we must pray for the Yankees that desire to restore the foundation of their federal government. Whenever we are able, we should also give them financial support and protection when it is necessary. We should pray for our Yankee brothers and sisters in Christ, just as we should pray for our brothers and sisters in Christ throughout the world. I should point out to you that when the government of the Republic is restored, the United States government must recognize the sovereignty of the constitution of the Confederate States of America within the Confederate States' borders. To deny this request is the deny the meaning and purpose of the Republic, for it was this Republic of the United States that was founded upon the documents of the constitution of the United States and from the Declaration of Independence.

Now! There are organizations who are working, at this very moment, to protect the small amount of liberties that still belong to the member states of the Union. They are working within the present system of government (Democracy) to protect the principles on which the United States was founded. The truth is that they are losing this war because the principles of the constitution of the United States are a contradiction to any other form of government (even a government form of Democracy). The constitution of the United States is a by-product of the NATURAL RIGHTS THAT GOD HAS GIVEN HUMANKIND. This is why the Confederate States had adopted this constitution of the United States, with some improvements, to be the foundation for their country. The constitution of the United States is a masterpiece that man has written upon a piece of paper. It did have a few minor flaws that needed to be cleared up. The fate and the future of the United States will depend upon the people who are true citizens within the member states of the union. The only way they can save their country is to have a restoration within their government, meaning: to restore the foundation of their government, which is the constitution of the United States. The first step is to restore the sovereignty to the union members' states governments. The second step is to dismember the Yankee Empire. The United States government, for such a long time, has been using the United States constitution as a smokescreen. They have been using the constitution by twisting the meaning of its statements to justify their power. Another way of putting it is to say that they are taking the letter of the law and distorting it in order to break the spirit of the law. This is why the Confederate States government felt that it was necessary to make some improvements within the document before it could become the constitution of the Confederate States of America.

Another form of political disease is Communism. People of North America have fallen for that propaganda lie saying that communism is dead, because they say that now the country of Russia is no longer a communist home base. Yet years ago Russia had planted the seed of communism within other countries. Communism was established here in North America sometime around the 1930s. The full force of communism did not take effect on the people of the United States and of the occupied Confederate States as it did in other countries. Nevertheless it did infiltrate the federal government and society. The Communist Party and the liberal party are just a few of those infiltrated. Democracy is like cocaine being laced with the acid of Communism. It is a quick way to kill someone with a drug problem. It is important for the people of the United States who desire to restore their country to the original foundations of the birth of the United States of America to be willing to pay the price of life and prosperity. They must also reach out to Christ and ask God to forgive them of their sins and the sins of their country. This must be done in order to restore the freedom they once had. They will have to be willing to pay a higher price for freedom than our founding Fathers did. The people of the Union should first try to have their people run for office and to hold every office that they can, from the Presidency down to the smallest office. Once they have their people in these positions, they should make the move to restore their government. If this does not work, they then have the right to rise up and take their government back under their control, even by force. If this is not the path they want to take, the last option they have is to have their state government withdraw their membership from the Union. In the eyes of the tyrants of Democracy this will be an act of treason. However, please remember that the Declaration of Independence does give this right to the people. In the eyes of our Heavenly Father and of our Founding Fathers, including our Confederate Forefathers, these are justifiable actions.

One of the greatest weapons the United State government has in its arsenal is the propaganda machine. It has been used to promote fear and hatred toward the Confederate people. It was used to promote the war effort upon the Confederate States of America. Statements such as these were used: to free the slaves, to save the Union from secessions, and to save the economy from the Confederate States' free trade. Propaganda is one of the tools that is used upon the people; and its starts in your public schools. The news media is another tool for the propaganda machine. Let us say that you were a Southerner and you had a desire to restore our countries' federal government and, in addition, the Confederate States Federal Government. Your desire is to restore our country's constitution of the Confederate States. You would believe that you were being a patriotic person who loves our country.

However once the propaganda machine is through with you, you will be classified as someone who is a racist, a bigot, or even a traitor. If you are from the Union and you have the desire to restore you country's government back to being a Republic, and if in addition you recognized the Confederate States of America as a separate country and are being a patriotic person, then you just might be classified as being a Right Wing fanatic or even a traitor. If you are from either country and want to restore your own country back to being a Christian society, then you might be classified as a religious fanatic or a cult member. Tyranny was much heavy at the time of the southern states secession, so much so that they felt that it was needful for them to withdraw from the union. In fact, it was even heavier than when the colonies were under the tyranny of Great Britain. In truth, we are living under much more tyranny today, at this very moment, than during the unconstitutional invasion of our land by the United States in 1861. The people in North America have become like sheep. They are always directed by the sheep dogs of military force.

Moreover the slaughter of the House of Democracy and the tyranny that follows it is never too far from the herd. The people of the United States and of the occupied Confederate States have become a gullible and a naive people. They have lost their identity as a people and as a true country. They have also lost the understanding of what real liberty is all about. They have become two countries that are lost in the wilderness of darkness. . . the blind leading the blind . . . quick to abandon the principles and the values of the foundation of freedom so that they may go and chase after false and shiny ideas that are filled with poison. A candy apple can have a perfect shape and a beautiful color of red, but it can also have a special surprise hidden within: a sharp razor blade. This is how quickly liberty can be lost. It can be taken from you, not long after you have fought and bled to earn it.

Let us say there was a child with a very special gift in his hand. In addition, that gift is the gift that guarantees that child's freedom. Then a stranger wants to take the gift from that child. What would the stranger do? First, the stranger would try to talk the child out of it; but if the child's reply is "NO!", then that same stranger will request that the child give it to him. If the child still comes back with the same reply: "NO!", the stranger will start to demand that the child give him the gift. The child will suddenly pull back and hold the gift closer to him and once more say "NO!". Then the stranger comes up with a great idea! He turns around and walks away, heading toward a toy store about two blocks away. After about 30 minutes, the stranger returns to speak to the child; and he says to the child, "I have something very special for you." Then he pulls his hand out of his pocket; and in his hand, he has a rubber ball. The ball is blue with shiny glitter on it. As the light from the sun shines up it, it has a glowing look. The child is amazed by the appearance of the shining object. He reaches out to take the shiny ball and the stranger suddenly pulls his arm back. The child is surprised by the stranger's reaction. Then the stranger says to the child, "I will make a trade with you. Give me the gift in you hand, and I will give you the ball." The child does as he asks; and the stranger starts to laugh. He said to the child, as he is smiling, "You can keep the ball and play with it for as long as you like. Nevertheless, from this day forward, you belong to me. You will think as I tell you to think. You will do as I tell you to do. In addition, you will belong to me until the end of your time."

This is what has happened to the United States, as well as to other countries. Moreover, this is also the result from the Yankee Empire, for it is the Confederate States who is suffering from the decisions and policies being in force here at home and throughout the world. It is true that Democracy is not as extreme as the communist form of government. Yet, all that communism is doing is taking it one step farther to the next level. One thing that Democracy and Communism have in common is the desire to rule the world; and they both believe that their way is best. They do not believe that the people have the right to choose the path that is best for them. Nevertheless to replace this government of the Republic with any other form of government is a direct mockery of the foundation of life, liberty, and the responsibility that goes along with it. This government was founded upon the Declaration of Independence and the Constitution of the United States of America and, most of all! The freedom of people to choose. Both Democracy and Communism deny these very rights and blessings that our Heavenly Father had given humankind. However, both Democracy and Communism do have the same enemy; and that, my friends, would be the Southern States of North America also know as The Confederate States of America. The Southern States have, for years, fought the policies of the socialist left and the deeper penetration of Democracy into the United States congress. They do so in order to protect the few rights our people have left. Moreover, most of the time they are outvoted. Most of the moral decay that is destroying our Confederate peoples' values, and causing the shame that our people have about themselves, comes from the foreign influence outside our Confederate borders. For years we have resisted this slow transition of the socialist left and the influence of its bed partner, Democracy. We can only pray that our Heavenly Father will come to our rescue to restore our Birth right as a sovereign country the Confederate States of America.

"The Illusion of the Union"

In the present state of today, that is during the time of writing this book, the people of the Union States and the States of the Confederacy have lost all reality regarding the true understanding of this simple word: The word "*liberty*" has become just as much an illusion to our minds, as has also the word "*Union*".

It has become a fact that some European countries know more about the truthful history of The War of the Northern Invasion than the present Southern people of the Confederate South.

The future fate of our Southern people has become a questionable thought because it has become very clear to me that North American history seems to be keeping pace with the changing of the seasons. It is true indeed that a people without a past shall, in the end, not have much of a future; and it is also sad to say that we are becoming a carbon copy of our Yankee conquerors.

In this world of reality, the simple truth must be told. This war was more than The War Between The States. It was a war that affected many issues; and it shall be, in the end, the downfall of the Yankee Empire. It was also a war of idealism concerning the philosophy of the correct form of government. On one side you had the Federalist, who supported the ideas of centralism and democracy. On the other side, you had the Anti-Federalist, who supported the ideas of states' rights and of the republic.

The Anti-Federalist had won the first round; and the Constitution of the United States was formed. The government of the republic came into being, once the states came together and gave birth to that federal government. It seems, at that time, that the subject was closed; however, 75 years later history had proved them wrong. What might be the other issues I was talking about? Without going into a deep subject, I shall hit the highlights.

1. The Northern states value "Economics" as the top priority. The Southern states value "Moral Principles" as their top priority. To threaten one of these is enough to cause a war.

2. The Northern state cling more to the philosophy of secular humanism and try to establish this philosophy in their society; however, the Southern states cling more to the philosophy of the Gospel of Jesus Christ, and we try to establish this in our society.

3. The Northern states are never content with the creation of God, and they strive to undo everything. The Southern states accept the creation of God as it is and believe that it is wiser to be content and work with nature instead.

4. The Northern states consider their culture to be the present. The Southern states consider their culture to be in the past, "their roots".

5. While the Northern states see the future in itself as improving the perfection of mankind, the Southern states see it as being the reverse.

6. As the Northern states see the human mind to be the center within mankind, the Southern states see the spirit self that dwells within each of us as the center of man.

Now I must bring you back to the end results of that great victory for the United States. Once the great states of the Union defeated our beloved Confederacy, they had, in reality, denounced the sovereignty of the Northern states' government. They had sole their birthright and trampled upon the Declaration of Independence and their U.S. Constitution in order to save the Union – a Union that cannot be saved by military force and surely not by socialist engineering. The last hope for the Union was lost once more Union troops were sent into South Carolina, to Fort Sumter, to us Southerners. You do not have to pull your pistol out of your holster to make us understand your intentions. All you have to do is unsnap your holster, and we will know where you're coming from. Propaganda had played a great role over the states of Union; and this propaganda program is being played upon all of the people within North America at this time.

The struggle to maintain the Federal Government of the Republic, as it was originally written within the Constitution of the United States of America, had slowly ground down to a no-win situation for the Southern states of the Union, not only because of the problem with the balance of voting power within the government, but also because the states of the North had become infected with the French Revolution for democracy.

Democracy is not a word that will be found within the U.S. Constitution, nor can the United States function as a democracy and still call itself a republic.

Even to this very day the so-called leaders within the federal government will vote on bills and projects that are unconstitutional. Every time someone votes for a bill that the Constitution of the United States does not give them the power to enforce, treason has been committed once more against the people. The federal government is not, nor has it ever been, nor shall it ever be, the voice of the people.

It is the state governments who spoke on behalf of the people of each state, not only before the writing of the Constitutions of the United States of America of the Confederate States of America, but also after these constitutions were written. Who is the voice of the people? Is it the news media? Is it Wall Street? No! It is the freedom of the press and the voting booth.

Ever since the United State invaded Confederate soil, the press has been used to control or regulate the amount of information and/or the kind of information the people are allowed to hear and know. The media has been used much like a cattle prod in order to direct the people in the direction that they want them to go. Movies from Hollywood are used in the same way: to promote and to influence people. Socialism, democracy, and secular humanism are the main tools that are used against the states of the Union and of the Confederacy.

Usually, when the United States government makes a statement to the people, it is on a "need-to-know" basis, or limited because of supposed "endangerment to national security". In most of these cases, it is more than likely that it regards something unconstitutional, to benefit the Yankee empire. So, when it comes to the media, we see what they want us to see; we hear what they want us to hear; and we know what they want us know. To them, there is no profit in the truth.

John T. Nall 9 May 2001

The Constitution

1. The Constitution that was approved by the States' Governments was nothing more than a verbal agreement that was established in writing, as a contract, in order to protect the sovereignty of each of the countries which are known as states; to specify what powers the federal government has and can legally enforce; and to stand together in times of danger at any given time that one of these member states has been invaded by a unwelcome nation.

2. Just as any other document, as long as those members who are the states joined together in order to protect each others' interest stand together in strength, continuing to abide by that constitution. Only by doing so shall that document be able to guarantee the correct amount of power that was established in the constitution.

3. If one member of the state continually violated the constitution, then by all rights the members of those states forming the Union or Confederacy should be able to vote to remove that state from their membership and from the protection of that document. This is something that our founding and Confederate forefathers did not think of at that time. However, if the federal government established itself over the constitution or even tried to do so, then it would have committed treason by violating that document, because it was that constitution that brought the federal government into being.

I'll put it to you like this: The constitution is designed to regulate the flow of power to specific areas of each party. Now, if a breach took place and a branch of government that was created by the constitution were to overstep its boundary for power, then it would fall upon the member states to regain that power that was guaranteed to them from that document that they had established. However, if the members were unable to restore that which was established by the constitution, then that same document would become null and void, the reason being that the constitution was designed to be regulated by the states for the security and liberty of all of the citizens from each state.

But let me tell you about the side of history of which you've never heard. If you were to take a stone and throw it into the middle of the pond, you would cause a ripple effect that would start from the middle and work its way to the outer banks of the pond. This is what happened to the true form of liberty, once Union troops were sent in to reinforce Fort Sumter, with the full knowledge that this was an act of aggression by the United States. The state of South Carolina was pushed into a situation in which self-defense was her only option; and as the freedom-loving Southerners they were, they fired the first shot! One bit of Yankee propaganda that you've heard so often over the years was that the Southern states had committed treason when t hey withdrew from the Union. It was also said that if states left the Union, then other states would follow and the country would crumble. However, this was a Yankee lie for the purpose of putting fear into the hearts of the Northern people and to gain their support in the effort to make war on the Confederate States of America.

The truth was that the constitution was no longer protecting the interest and safety of these Southern states. For one thing, the balance of power had shifted into the control of the Northern states; and the Southern states were paying, and are still paying to this day, heavy taxation without representation. And let us not forget the first terrorist group that was born in North America: the abolitionist organization which took pleasure in murderous acts toward families and destruction of private property. And all the while the federal government took their sweet time to come to the rescue.

Basically, this is my understanding of the Yankee train of thought: "This Union has become like the Mafia; and the only way you can leave is feet first", or to join the Union would be like saying that we had signed that contract in blood. Point of fact: Liberty is the foundation of a true government. The government and everything else is built upon that foundation; but once the foundation becomes unstable, then the government no longer serves the needs of the people. It begins to become a question of who should be serving who.

What is a nation? The first thing we must understand is that a nation is not based on the size of the territory or the population of that area. A nation is born when all of these goals fall into the proper place: 1) A selfsufficient government that can provide and protect the safety and liberty with the responsibility that God has given it. 2) That it was the will of the people to establish that government; and 3) that the blood of the people has been spilled in order to defend and protect that nation.

But please let me clear your mind of the Yankee myth of: Your country is your government! Regardless of whether or not it is the state or federal government, it is in truth the place which your state government represents. It is the federal government that represents the interest of the states and nothing more. However, when the federal government no longer represents the interest and safety of the states and is no longer bound by the constitution that was established by the states, then my dear friends, this is when treason is afoot!

As it was established by our Founding Fathers, each state is a separate and a sovereign country or nation. Some may ask you just how many states it takes to create a country. Some may say "13"; others may say "50"! But the truth is that it only takes one. It was the states who fought for independence. It was the states who created the federal government in order that the sovereignty of each state should be protected from outside invasion. State rights are still as sovereign as they were before the creation of the federal government.

Sovereignty was guaranteed in the constitution that was drafted by those same states. I say this because it was the powers of the federal government that were regulated within that constitution and not the other way around. To deny the withdrawal of a state from a corrupt system is to deny the sovereignty of that state. It is the same as saying that the state does not exist.

It is no more treason to withdraw from the Union than it was to withdraw from Great Britain. To say otherwise would be a lie.

I find it strange that people say that it was the Southern states that committed treason. For the question is just how much tyranny is acceptable before the people stand forth and strike back or step away and start all over. And you should think about it like this: A tyrant never thinks himself to be someone of that nature; and even a government can fall under that same spell. Blind as some people are, they will cling to tyranny and hold it tightly to their hearts. They may do it for many reasons: 1) fear, 2) loyalty, 3) denial, 4) greed, 5) ignorance.

Our Nation's Heritage

Heritage is a special and important thing for a people. It becomes the very building block of a people and Country. It is the explanation to the identification of a people's birthright. In addition, it is a way of life that is defining in how everything is related, to them and to their way of living. This is the glue which give them the desire to stand together and to fight for each other as a people. Heritage is something that every tyrant and every Empire is afraid of. For when a people have their heritage, it becomes clear that their loyalty will not yield to anything that would be a contradiction to it. Heritage is everything that has an effect within your daily lives. Heritage plays just as much on a person's personality. It becomes clear that there are two important ingredients that people need in their lives: (1) to know and understand who they are within the physical realm as a person and as a people; (2) to know who they are and the meaning and value of life within the spiritual realm. Heritage is the actuality that can bring forth good or bad fruit in our actions and decisions. A people without their heritage is transformed into the living dead, zombies that can be easily influenced and controlled by the voodoo magic of lies and emotional war tactics. To strip away the heritage of a people is to cause an implosion that can seal the end fate of a people and country. Indeed, you would be able to use these people as your mindless army of zombies for a short time; however the bomb would eventually tick down to zero. Then the fate of that people would be sealed forevermore.

This is not important, however, to those who play with people's lives just for their own personal gain. Our Confederate Heritage or Southern Heritage, if you will, is blended with the best qualities of different nationalities and of races. If you were to break down our Confederate Heritage, you would find history leading to the Celtic, Native Indians, and Africans. If you searched even further, you could even find the influence of Hebrew, Spanish, and French, as well. Some influences might have been greater than others but it is all the same to us. Our society had a balance between integration and segregation of the Southern peoples. At times, we might struggle with one another over different issues and beliefs. Nevertheless, when danger is near, we put our differences to the side and stand together (as Southern people). We do not believe in fixing anything that is not broken; and we are slow to anger. However, we are very protective when it comes to our liberty and the way we should treat others. We are a cautious people, who wait to see the big picture before we devote our word to it. These were some of the things that we, as Southerns, once were. Increasingly as each generation of our people steps forward, we are more foreign to the generation that comes after us. In addition, with the flooding of illegal aliens into our Country, including the Yankees, we could eventually become deluded and become something that is worse than death. That would be non-Southern and non-Confederate: strangers to our past and foreign to our ancestors, the very by-product of liberty that has been crushed and condemned by the Yankee Empire.

We are not a perfect people; and we are also guilty of being sinners in the eyes of our God. But we do not believe that the Yankees quality to sit on the throne of God and throw stones at our glass house, telling us how we should run our State governments and our personal lives. In fact, they need to be down on their knees beside us, asking for forgiveness from our Creator. In addition, the last thing we want is to see the Yankees destroy their own Country and fall into our laps once more. There are some Yankees who are good people and have respect for us as Southerners and Confederates. We would not mind if they wanted to live with us. However, we do not want the whole Yankee tribe or Nation to come down and take control over the little amount of freedom that we have, including taking our land and women.

Once, when I was at work, a woman from the countryside of New York State told me that the problem with the South is that it is too Southern and too religious. That offended me and hurt my feelings. After the conversation was over, she came back later and apologized to me for her remarks; however, during the conversation, she said that everything down here is the same and that we are not as diversified in everything, as it is in her State. She said that she has lived in North Carolina for 16 years and she is tired of the same old lifestyle of the south. She is tired of the restaurants serving her grits instead of bagels. I had to take some time to think about what she said; and I later went back to her and told her that the problem she is having is not so much with us Southerners. The problem is that she does not like the grass to grow underneath her feet, and she gets bored with life too easily. Nevertheless, it is stupid for me to go out to the Western States of North America, tell those people that they are too Western, and expect them to change just for my sake. It would be just as wrong and disrespectful for me to go into the Country of Japan and tell them that they are too Japanese and need to diversity. The truth is, I believe that we have gone too far in this diversity dung. We need to return to the roots of our southland and lifestyle.

Our Confederate people must become like the seed of a mighty oak tree. We must stand tall, strong, and never lean in the direction of emotions, diversity, and transformation of the blowing of the wind. Unlike the wheat that is in the fields, some bend to the wind without self-determination and will power. If the wind becomes too strong, or if someone steps on them, they may not rise and return to their original stance. Indeed, do they not look beautiful when the wind is blowing through the fields? They lean to the left and then to the right; but what is the life span of the wheat compared to the oak tree?

The reality is that the Federalist and the Socialist left have become tired of hearing our battle cry for freedom. They brush away the notion of the Southland being a separate Nation and sweep it under the rug. They are determined to put our Southern or Confederate Heritage and symbols somewhere in a museum. This way, they can be forgotten and mocked at by passers by. They proclaim that it is not proper to fly our battle flag of the Confederacy; however, they claim, it is proper to fly that ugly candy cane Federalist banner on our Southern soil. Someone once said that "first, they will go after the battle flag, and next will be the Christian cross". The fact is that Christianity is already under attack. In addition, the downtreading of the battle flag of the Confederacy is just the beginning of things to come. The truth is that they do not like the idea of throwing a stick and having us refuse to run after it and give it back to them. The one thing that Yankees have not learned is this: Heritage is not something that you put on a shelf, thinking of the good old days that are long past. It is not a faded something based on materialism or some sort of mood swing. In a way, it becomes a genetic code or a tightknit people that make a Country or a nation. It is the one common denominator enabling people of different races to embrace each other without having to commit genocide towards others or themselves. Since Christianity is the water that is added to a mixture of sand that we call our Heritage, this cement does become a solid foundation for a colorful people and Country. Heritage is a way of life that we live our lives by. It never changes or is to be discarded. It is a road map that was meant to be given to the next generation and the generations following them. It is not so much a tradition as it is a fingerprint of our Southern or Confederate people.

Our Confederate people have become like a shake and bake society. We have become a people that have gotten lost in a House of Mirrors, a carnival sideshow that can only be found in the middle of the twilight zone. The images that we see of ourselves become lost in this dream state of the Yankeedom of Oz. It is time for us to rediscover our past and find our roots. Our Heritage is the very reflection of our shadow, a shadow that is never too far away and is always connected to our feet.

Our heritage is a past that helps us to rediscover ourselves as a people and as individuals; a treasure box filled with moments of our past, like pictures of a story that has not found its ending. It can help us refocus our destiny in this mad, mad world, to fine-tune ourselves as a people. Just as it is necessary to fine-tune an instrument now and then, we need a reality check from our hearts up to our heads, a treasure map of heritage that guides us toward our final destination and prevents us from falling into the same booby traps that our ancestors found. Our heritage is a safety protocol, that guides us safely along our journey. Our history is also a testimony of the just and of the injustice of those who went before us. Our Heritage and history serves many different purposes. It helps us to walk in the steps of grandeur, prevents us from stepping into those same steps of failure into which our people have fallen in the past. It is a road sign that protects us from following other roads that have led different people into a world of hallucinations of total equality in every aspect of their lives. It is a blessing from our God to us, so that we may forget not of whom we are and what we are as a Southern people and as a Confederate Nation. It is the final ribbon, which has been wrapped around a gift. That gift, the legacy of our people and Country, was given in order that we may be able to hand it down into the hands of the next generation.

Some of our people would like to believe that the past has no value and meaning in their present and future state of being. They have been kept in the closet of ignorance. Brushing off the past is a quick way to avoid looking stupid and admitting that they have no idea what you are talking about. For others, living within an invisible bubble , they refuse to believe anything else that is outside the realm of their personal lives. Being selfcentered is another way of putting it. The truth is this: the past is in reality a force of power that only the people can harness and use as a source of light. Moreover, we were meant to take that light as a tool, and use it to penetrate the darkness ahead of us, to carry with us on our journey into the future. Not only was it meant to remid us who we are, but also to protect us from harm's way. To make this very clear for y'all to understand this very last statement: it is the final cornerstone, which is put in its place once the foundation of liberty has been laid down for our people and Country.

Because it is that cornerstone, it gives extra strength to that foundation. What is it that we are building on top of this foundation? It is our future, the future of our people and Nation. If you shook the foundation, then everything on top of it just might fall. We have been having earthquakes ever since Union forces occupied our Confederate soil. These earthquakes are getting stronger as time passes. Eventually they will become so strong that they will start to split the foundation into broken pieces of stone and dust. Being a conquest of this Imperialism of Federation is playing a perilous game of Russian roulette with our foundation and our Confederation. It may soon be the death of us all.

Ever since the invasion and occupation of our Country, our people have been put in the category of second class citizens. Our land is being used as unlimited resources by the occupier. They also find us Southerns below their idea of perfection. They would prefer that we vanish or fade away, while leaving everything behind for them. However, they do not mind if our people go into these wars of theirs and fight on behalf of the Yankee Empire. When the word Southerner comes to the minds of Yankees, they see us as being related to the cartoon of Goofy, created by Walt Disney. They especially view of mountain people in this way. The rest of us Southerners are looked down on as being rednecks or some other stupid name like that. They would like to believe that our gene pool is filled with impurities. At the same time, they would like to believe that somehow they are higher up on the food chain. It just might even bring more fear to them to learn that Heaven will have a large number of Southerners. In addition, we will still be speaking with our Southern accent. It is a wonderful thing to know whether a Yankee can make it to heaven and still care not for us, having to listen to us for all eternity. I am sure this won't be a problem for our other Yankee brothers and sisters in Christ, who will be with us.

We do not mind having non-Southerners as friends, provided that they are not hostile, nor trying to transform us into some ungodly worldly view of utopia and miscegenation. Some of us might even treat some of these Yankee friends as part of the family. I am sure that the federal government of the United States does not want the people to know that some Yankees fought for the Confederacy and wore the Grey. Those Yanks in Grey fought for the Confederate States not only because of their love for the Southern people, but also because they had a better understanding of what a Republic was meant to be. Now their Yankee tribe might consider them traitors. However, those Yanks in Grey believed that it was the other way around. So do not be surprised to run into a Yank that has a Confederate spirit within.

Nor should we forget those Confederate Yanks who might have fought for our Nation and states. I hope that there will be more research done on this and that it will become a subject found in our Confederate history. The one thing that our people must understand is this: whenever the federal government is speaking to the public about "fighting for our freedom", they are in truth speaking about the freedom of government from being restrained, from their United States Constitution of bondage.

I do not want to be mean about this! Nevertheless, it is time for us to wean the people of North America off their milk and cookies. In reality, we are not and do not live in the land of the free and the home of the brave, since the federal storm troopers overtook our Nation's Capitol of Richmond, Virginia. In addition to causing our Federal government of the Confederacy to disperse and be unable to regroup, freedom for both of our countries burst into flames and tumbled back toward the Earth, crashing into the dust. The quest to advance the liberties of both of our great Nations shattered as quickly as a high sound wave, which can penetrate a glass of wine and cause the wine to stain the ground in red. It was a quick death blow to the head for true liberty. Nevertheless, we must stand together as Christians and as Confederates, uncompromising in our principles nor sacrificing our liberty, as has been defined by our heritage.

It is said that we should not live in the past and we must cling to the present. This present, not of our legacy will lead us on a one way ticket to a highway to hell. The Yankees cannot seem to understand why we have a strong dislike for them! I am sure that a lot of them didn't come to the United States until long after the Yankee invasion. Most Yankees have no idea what really took place during that time. The only things they have to go by would be those propaganda manuals that they call history books, the same propaganda manuals that are found in Federation camps, or, if you like, reconstruction camps. I do not think that I am able to clarify this more to y'all. But let me put it in another way. Since constitutionally we are no longer voluntary members in that Union, then we are a Confederate people of the southland have no moral or constitutional obligation to duty to interfere or take part within the States of the Union or of its federal government. However, I would like to suggest that we send Christian missionaries to the States of the Union.

Let me tell you why we still have some dislikes for their country and our illegitimate Uncle Sam.

1. Our federal government of the Confederate States has never surrendered or signed any peace treaty with the United States, meaning that the war is not over, but has only transformed into other tactical forms.
2. Forcing the States of the Confederacy to repay the United States in taxes for their war effort that they, the United States, inflicted on the Confederacy.
3. Reconstruction 1 and 2.
4. For violating the constitutional rights of the Southern states after their secession from the Union and forcing the State of South Carolina to defend herself against the unwelcome Union troops that had crossed her State borders.
5. For denying our Southern States of the Confederacy the right of self-determination and treating the Southern people as a second class, subject to the Empire.
6. For polluting our culture and society with their Democracy and secular humanism.
7. For establishing Union military bases on Confederate soil, without the permission of the State Governments, including our federal government of the Confederate States, which should be in power and active at this very moment.
8. For using those Union federalist military bases to enforce their will on other countries, even when it became a violation of their own constitution of the United States.
9. For overriding a state's constitution and using the federal storm troopers as military muscle.
10. For causing racial strife by putting the color of a person's skin into a voting block. In addition, for causing a vacuum of emptiness that became filled with white supremacy and its fascism.
11. For giving fascism an open door for non-fascism to embrace the doctrine of socialism.
12. For using Yankee Negro troops to punish and persecute the Southern people for leaving the Union. In addition, for using Southern Negroes as puppets, as a punishment for the Southern whites, as it was this that started the racial strife between the Confederate people of different races.
13. For rejecting the Gospel of Jesus Christ and rejection of the foundation of Christianity, on which the federal government had been founded.
14. For persecuting a Christian child, who will practice Christian beliefs, within the public school system.
15. For persecuting Confederate children for having or wearing anything with a Confederate battle flag thereon.
16. For intentional committing of racial genocide toward all of the Confederate people during their invasion. For promoting racial genocide toward all Southerners of race with miscegenation. For enforcing racial genocide toward all Southerners of race by using and enforcing abortion

centers for the method of population control. For promoting and protecting the practice of homosexuality within the Confederacy.
17. For pushing the Confederacy into a third world country status and preparing the Confederate states for the one world government.
18. For taking over the rights of the parents and claiming all children as property of the state.

These are only a few of the things that I can think of at this time. However, I am sure that you could think of more for yourself. To continually believe that the federal government of the New United State of Democracy cares and desires to protect our Southern people is not only foolish, but is an act of denial. History is a reminder of the blood of our Confederate people dripping from their Federalist Yankee banners the blood of the victims, that the United States has spilled, from every Southerner of race up until this present time in our lives. War crimes, that people never hear about, have been committed against our Country and other Countries around the world, by the United States. History has proven that regardless of how great and noble a Country may be, as soon as it becomes a centralized power or a world power Nation it automatically starts to deteriorate and decay from within. North America has fallen into a state of tunnel vision. They have lost their perspective on how the past affects the future. They cannot see anything of the past or how it can have an effect on the future. They only care to live in the present and care not of the consequences that it could have in the future. People have been preconditioned not to question, wonder, or even to compare the teachings that they receive in federal government schools. They are quick to accept the present as a natural result of what their Country and liberty are all about. Most of them do not have the backbone to restore that freedom that was meant for our children by our Founding Fathers and Confederate ancestors. They are afraid of losing everything that they have and of going to jail. They are afraid for the safety of their loved ones. Until they are willing to lose everything they have, including their own lives, they understand not the meaning of freedom.

It is easy to celebrate Independence Day, a reminder of your country's ancestry. It is easy to wear uniforms worn by your ancestors and to play the role. But it means nothing to the people of the past, present, and future, unless you pick up the banner and the ideas that it represents and make a stand in your own shoes. The flag of liberty is not a banner that is to be laid down after the war. It is not a changing symbol, despite the outcome of a war. It is not just a symbol of the past, for it is also a hope for the future. It is to be handed down from our generation to the next, in the name of liberty, for that banner is our Confederate States Third National.

Some people believe that just because they or a family member fought in a war that this is a symbol of freedom. I must say that they are very wrong on this point. If your State's Constitution or your Federal Constitution were in danger from within, and in peril of being eliminated, then you would be fighting for freedom. If war were to break out in order to protect the citizens of your member states, then you would be fighting for freedom. However, if war breaks out because of fighting over control of materials and resources, because of the mistakes of your political leaders, for the gain of more governmental power and land, if the military is used for policing and controlling other Countries, these things would not be fighting for freedom. Your freedom is not your Federal or State government. Your freedom is your State and Federal Constitutions and your relationship with God through His Son Jesus Christ. It does not matter if your Federal or State government crumbles into dust from conquest or from neglect. They can always be rebuilt. Nevertheless, do not ever lose the constitutions of your State and Federal government, for it is these two the define the freedom for your people and Country.

If you believe in fighting for your federal government, then you are an enemy of liberty and of freedom, for a Federal Government does not always have the people's best interest at heart. The Federal Government is like a two – year – old toddler, with the people as its parents. The toddler is always testing its parents to see just how much it can get away with. Therefore you must always keep your eyes and ears open and on guard. You must be forever hearing and never let the toddler out of your sight. It has never been the will of our Founding and Confederate forefathers for the Federal government to outgrow and become the master over the people and its member States. As a parent, you have a voice to vote and give your point of view. Should it become necessary for you to discipline your child, you must bear arms and put the toddler in its proper place. The only time you should discipline the toddler is when it (the Federal Government) turns deaf ears to you and when it is overriding the Federal constitution.

The Federal government is like a cobra in a basket. If you are careful and know what you are doing, you can open the basket, let the cobra stick its head out, and be able to control it. However, as soon as you take your eyes off it, you are suddenly bitten, and then you will die. Being cautious and a little paranoid is a natural state for a people who understand the meaning of freedom. I am sure you have heard that old adage "beware of wolves in sheep's clothing". In order to catch a wolf in sheep's clothing, you must first look within the flock of sheep. If the wolf was on the outside of the herd, it would look like the rest of the wolf pack. You cannot protect your flock from the dangers outside until you know your flock is safe from within. If you are not cautious and a little paranoid, you just might end up being the main course of the meal, lamb chops and gravy with creamed potatoes on the side. To walk blindly without a care in the world and only care about your little bubble that you call a life is not just leaving the door open for people with evil hearts to rule over you and your family, it leaves the door open for those same people to rule over your people as well. Some people seem to think that the liberty our Confederate people once had under the Constitution of the Confederate States, including the liberty that the Federalist people once had under the Constitution of the United States, is something that you can pick up at a fast food restaurant. In fact, they believe that liberty is supposed to be recyclable like paper. They can use it whenever they want to and later toss it to the side as trash. My dear friends of liberty, this is not the case!

The Offence Of That Symbol

The battle flag of the Confederate States of America is a symbol which the United State media proclaims to be controversial. The question as to why remains. The problem that we are seeing in the federalist government public school is the negative reactions of Confederate Negroes toward any Confederate Caucasians wearing clothing with the Confederate flag thereon. The reason that the flag becomes offensive to the black folks is because of the false teachings that the children are receiving from those government schools. The Confederate Negroes have been denied the truth about their true identity and heritage just as our white folks have been denied. Therefore they believe that the Confederate flag is a symbol of oppression and of pro-slavery. Why does the United State fear this symbol so much? Well, let's look at the meaning behind the flag.

1. The battle flag is also a military flag that represents the military forces of the Nation of the Confederate States of America.
2. The battle flag therefore is a symbol of that Nation's federal government. (*A Constitutional Republic*).
3. The battle flag is a flag of liberty. Therefore it is anti-Democracy, anti-Fascism, and anti-Communism, as well as *anti* any other form of government that would be a contradiction to its government's Constitution.
4. The battle flag is also a symbol of Christianity. Therefore it stands against the spiritual forces and influences of the prince of darkness.

Therefore, we can see why, after all of these years, the United State government still has hatred toward our Nation's military banner. It dares to defy the will of the Democracy of the United State of America. The battle flag is a reminder that we are a sovereign Nation that is occupied by them. It is a reminder to them also of the government that our Founding Fathers meant to always have. It is also clear that the Communist Party understands this all too well and has the determination to destroy the integrity and character of our Confederate Nation and people.

Our children of this generation are struggling to define the meaning of themselves as individuals and as a people. They are persecuted in the indoctrination Federalist camps for wearing anything that has a Confederate emblem on it. They are denied the freedom to practice their Christianity in their daily lives during the course of their school hours. And some of them are willing to be murdered first rather than deny our Lord God. They are indeed the Spirit Of The Confederacy. Those that are offended by symbols of our Confederacy are being offended by their own ignorance. How can a person understand the meaning of the truth when the only thing that they have ever known is a lie?

Psalms 2: 1-10

KING JAMES BIBLE

Why do the heathen rage,
and the people imagine a vain thing?
The kings of the earth set themselves,
and the rulers take counsel together,
against the LORD,
and against His anointed, *saying*,
Let us break their bands asunder,
and cast away their cords from us.
He that sitteth in the heavens shall laugh:
the LORD shall have them in derision.
Then shall He speak unto them in His wrath,
and vex them in His sore displeasure.
Yet have I set My King
upon My holy hill of Zion.
I will declare the decree:
the LORD hath said unto me,
Thou *art* My Son;
this day have I begotten Thee.
Ask of Me,
and I shall give *Thee* the heathen
for thine inheritance,
and the uttermost
parts of the earth *for* thy possession.
Thou shalt break them
with a rod of iron;
and thou shalt dash them in pieces
like a potter's vessel.
Be wise now therefore, O ye kings:
be instructed, ye judges of the earth.

Serve the LORD with fear,
and rejoice with trembling.
Kiss the Son, lest he be angry, and ye perish *from*
the way , when his wrath is kindled but a little.
Blessed *are* all they that put their trust in him.

CONFEDERATE FLAG

1998

LIVING BIBLE

What fools the nations are to rage against the Lord!
How strange that men should try to outwit God!
For a summer conference of the nations has been called
to plot against the Lord and his Messiah,
Christ the King
"Come, let us break his chains," they say,
"and free ourselves from all this slavery to God."
But God in heaven merely laughs!
He is amused by all their puny plans.
And then in fierce fury he rebukes them and fills them with fear.
For the Lord declares,
"This is the King of my choice,
and I have enthroned him in Jerusalem, my hold city."
His chosen one replies,
"I will reveal the everlasting purposes of God, for the Lord has said to me,
'You are my Son.
This is your Coronation Day. Today I am giving you your glory." "Only ask and I will give you
all the nations of the world. Rule them with an iron rod; smash them like clay pots!"
O kings and rulers of the earth, listen while there is time.
Serve the Lord with reverent fear; rejoice with trembling.
Fall down before his Son and kiss his feet before his anger is roused and you perish.
I am warning you – his wrath will soon begin.
But oh, the joys of those who put their trust in him!

"To Have Eyes and Yet To Be Blind"

God is not a God based on the perception of man; however, he is a spiritual being who goes far beyond the expectations of mankind. His actions do not just bring glory upon Him, for it is the glory which mankind should give to Him; but He is teaching us that it is in Him alone that all things begin. He is the Creator who always goes the extra length to prove His point.

At times, His actions may serve to accomplish different things at once. He cannot become a contradiction to Himself and for being that which He is, the spiritual and the natural gateway of life. Both come to benefit from His presence. By working only within the realm of Christianity, He has stepped to the side when it comes to the rest of the world. He is giving this world enough time to create the history of mankind who have not chosen His way.]

This history of this world shall be the conviction of the testimony against those who have chosen to be their own God. As William Shakespeare once put it, "The world is a stage, and we are merely the players." In many ways, He has given us many insights into His presence, just by being within the gateway of the natural world.

The reason that mankind is unable to understand who (Jehova our God) truly is the simple truth that they refuse to accept the fact that they are a creation instead of being the creator. Atheists are the ones who are truly lost, because they don't really understand the true picture of the evolution of man. The evolution of mankind is not based on the physical area of man; however, evolution is based on the relationship between the spirit that is within you and our Heavenly Father, only through His Son, who is our Messiah and our true King.

To be unconditionally faithful to Christ and His Father is accomplished through His Holy Spirit's enabling us to live by His word. As His word becomes our life, we become the living Bible, or the living word. It is through the Father, the Son, and the Holy Ghost, that we gain the evolution of spiritual growth.

Spiritual sin is, in truth, the evolution in reverse. As cancer is a disease to your body, so sin is a disease to your spirit. The end result will lead to death. The views on the evolution of atheism are a failure; and I can give you two reasons: (1) Evolution of the flesh has no meaning, because in the end your body will turn to dust. (2) Technology is not wisdom. Unlike Adam, the reason that we cannot use the full force of our minds is because of sin. If we had, the world would have ended a long time ago! Think about how much damage we have done with the small portion that we have used with our mental powers.

By the lack of understanding of the true meaning of God, the only concept that most of mankind has about Him is that He is a being who creates something from nothing. However, He is much more! He wants to make it clear that not only is He the One and Only True God, but there is none other like

Him. So what He has done is to put the answers within His Creation; and the answers are the every kind of its kind.

Meaning that the creation of that which is the only kind, then it goes into every kind of that kind, the same species of a different variety. He has done this not just with that of the living, but also with that which is not. No two planets are the same. Yet they are both planets. No two snowflakes are the same, yet they are snowflakes.

Now I am going to cover a subject that most people don't want to hear. When it comes to that which is of the living, there is something about everyone of its kind that makes it special and unique in its own way, for each and every race of man. Each one has something about them that makes them superior and inferior to another race. There is no such thing as a superior race. The word race is nothing more than the variety of mankind.

The next level after that is the sexes. Every man has something that makes him superior and inferior next to a woman. God has broken this down to where each person has qualities about them that fall in the same category. This doesn't begin to cover the different cultures and languages, etc., the balance of the cycle of Father Creation and how everything fits together just like a puzzle. You would think that people would step outside of their homes and look around them and see the fingerprints of God; but most do not!

And so you begin to question where the meaning of equality comes in and what does it mean? Equality was given to us by our Heavenly Father. It cannot be created by man's own will; and He has covered this is many areas.

1. Love the Lord your God with all your heart (spirit) and with all of your soul (mind) and with all of your strength (body).
2. Love your neighbor as you love yourself.
3. Do to others as you would have them do unto you.
4. A nation that is not for God is a nation that is against Him; and if we do not use the liberties that He has given to a nation that is based on His word, then those liberties shall be taken away by others who are against Him. For this is the punishment that falls upon a society of that nation, which has fallen from God's grace.
5. Read Romans 12: 19 – 21.

What is the very truth that we have not yet come to understand? That it is Satan who is filled with envy! For he knows that he cannot take the place of God; and the very creation of God is a reminder to Satan that he is not and never will be a true God, because of the hatred that comes from his envy of God. It is his desire to wipe away the very evidence of the Fingerprints of the Creator. Once everyone and everything becomes equal in the thinking of Satan and of man, then where will we be able to see the variety of the glory of God's creation? But let us remember that this is only a stepping stone compared to what our eye of faith is in knowing who our true God is!

2 February 2000

Man's Evolution In Error

The theory of something that comes from nothing. And the theory that life came forth with a bang is something that we should question as to being the truth. For every action, there is a reaction. And every reaction changes the present time from the past. Life is not created from the bang theory, because an explosion can only destroy and not create. The creation of life and all of the surrounding things [the universe] has to come from a force of action and guidance in that direction. Only life is able to create life and is able to direct that force of energy of movement in order to create that which we would like to call life. Life is a continuation of itself that requires a balance of itself and everything that is around it. It is required to function this way so it can serve the purpose of the living. Life is unable to change itself at will because the atom is unable to contradict its functions. Time has no basis in the transformation of evolution of life because the atom is the same molecule as it was when it was created, the very blueprint of everything of the living and of the nonliving. The living is able to adapt in order to survive; and if it fails to adapt then it will surely die.

Of every living thing, there is a verity of each living thing. The world flood and the forces of nature destroyed that which was not destroyed by the hands of man. Thus these species that have died have been claimed to be the evolution of these species of the present life forms. If life was created by nothing and nothing has no action, then this can only mean that the purpose of life is nothing, and nothing is the fate for the meaning of life. It is impossible for the cycle of life and the relationship of the universe to be so perfect and to exist without some form of influence. The thought that life is always changing and is always improving itself without any guidance and without any purpose is not only illogical, but irrational as well. True science is to search for the answers about what and how life and our environment work in relation with itself. They can only present the truth that is founded on facts that they have found. To promote a theory of evolution without truthful evidence is to promote an idea as a religion so that one can control what they believe to be in their own minds to be the truth.

The Moral Conduct of Honor

1. Sin is not only a by-product of the end results of spiritual death! It also declines a human being to become more of the opposite of the true nature of being human. Man was made perfect by the glory of God; but once sin stepped between the Creator and His creation, the nature of man began to conduct himself in a unnatural way.

2. A person can live his life under the principles of moral conduct without this being a reflection of his heart. This is what we define as a Christian society, and by doing so, he conducts himself in a way that is close to the true nature of man.

3. The truest form of the reflection of man comes from the rebirth of his heart or spirit which reflects outwardly what also affects his natural self. Being a child of Christ becomes a natural way of life, which becomes more than a way, but *the* way one conducts himself.

4. As a non-Christian, the only honor that you have to protect is your family name. The way you conduct yourself and the value of keeping your word become a reflection of the respect or disrespect that others will have toward you and your family.

5. As a Christian, the only way to protect your family name is to protect the honor of the Name of Jesus Christ. The first reason is that all glory must go to God in everything that you do. The second reason is that it is the Blood of Christ, Who had covered your sins, that took place under your family name; and so a Christian has two family names that fall under his duty to protect: his spiritual name and his natural name. To protect one is to bring honor to the other.

6. It is far better for society and military to have leaders who are Christians because these Christians believe that their actions shall fall under the jurisdiction of the judgment of God. At the same time, with the help of Christ, they shall control or slow down the moral decay.

7. By doing so, the country and its military would have a better chance of having God to bless them, instead of His turning away. The best way to find a righteous leader is to judge his actions and his words. A righteous man is the same outside of the public's eye, when no one is around, or when he believes that no one is watching him. This is not someone who is perfect, but someone who strives to please the will of the Lord.

From Nothing Into Something

The concepts of the meaning of living our lives come from the understanding of where life began, to the meaning of our daily living, unto our future and the results that it will bring. To live our lives upon the bases of understanding that which is taught to us regardless if it is the truth or a lie including the amount of knowledge that is granted to us does play its part in the direction of the lives of all of mankind and Nations. It determines how we see ourselves and from that, how we see others that pass our way. In understanding the creation of all life and the history of mankind on this Earth, it all adds up to the history of life itself and the meaning and the value of it. The struggle to control that knowledge is the determination to control the fate of Mankind and the Nations thereof.

In order to first understand who we are as individuals, we must first learn whether or not we are a creation by force that gives reaction to the substance of all things. The second step is to learn who and why we have been created in that way and what is it that would establish a connection and a relationship with that creator, who is also known as **God of all creation**. The following step would be to learn or relearn about ourselves as a people and to finally take that last journey in our lifetime in knowing who we are as one self. These are the questions for which our children are seeking an answer, even when at times they may not know the questions to ask. Our universe was created to work within harmony and to coexist with all things within the boundaries of our universe. It is Mankind that can follow the flow and function in a positive direction that would not cause harm to this universe in which we live. But it is we, as mankind, that have been given the free will just as the angels in heaven to choose the pathway of good or evil and as a human species, to question and to ponder and to explore all things of ourselves and all that is around us.

The conclusion of understanding about oneself does not stop from the time that you are born, which is just beginning of that pathway of self-searching. As you go along the journey of life, it is during those very moments that you are learning about yourself, with every choice you make and every mistake that you overcome. Everything that takes place around you has an effect upon you as a person; but in our journey of self-searching you should know that you are of body and of spirit. It is your body that functions like a machine, but in the spirit you are of your true self and seeking to question the whom, where, when, AND what questions about yourself and life itself. The reason that children are filled with void in their spirit is the fact that the answers that they learn in public schools are false and misleading. Thus they try to find or create a personality that they can claim to be themselves, for if the world is not what they are told that it is, then they will reject everyone else who believe that it is so.

Unfortunately most parents may not know the real answers to these things. As human beings, we must first know the answers to some basic questions before we are able to discover what changes what we are to be in the end. Most of the time we will know if these answers are of sound foundation, because in our minds, we may believe in lie, but our spirits are unable to accept it to be the truth. So we tend to search for answers of our own. If we cannot find the answers, then we create our own personality to fill that void within us. Teenagers are able to understand more, without knowing why, that things are not as they should be, even after the parents have accepted things as they are. One of the reasons that Christianity has failed in reaching out to children is the fact that it has divided into denominations, for denominations do not accept all of the gospel as it is written and do not have the Holy Spirit to guide them in its understanding. They do not always practice what is written. Therefore a child left with only part of the answers to the riddle, and most of the time, it confuses them even more. To feel disconnected and lost or misplaced is the first reaction to the questions that will follow them; and the answers will determine what kind of personality they will have, because it is the first step in knowing who they are and how will affect them along the way. Our children and even adults need a role model that is perfect and is pure in every way. Someone they can strive to be like and who will help them to grow. Our spirits are starving for the food of understanding a need to change and grow for though we may become as adults, spiritually we are just children. Physically we will outgrow our parents, but spiritually we are seeking another, for only *Jesus Christ* is able to bring us to Him. For with Him, and the guidance of the Holy Spirit, we shall become as perfect as He wants us to be, not always perfect by our weakness, but of the heart and our faithfulness. *IN CHRIST, WE SHALL COME TO KNOW OURSELVES.*

Upside Down Cake

From the time that God gave Adam permission to rule over the Earth and to be caretaker of it, that responsibility fell upon all of Mankind to do the same, for the birth of Mankind began in the womb of Eve and the seed of Adam. This responsibility not only deals with the way we care for this Earth in the physical way, but it applies to a spiritual way as well. I say this because our God is a spiritual being and all of Mankind are spiritual beings within this physical realm. One may forget that at times, but it is true that this world is not the center of the universe. It is true that the planets do not revolve around our Earth. Yet this Earth is the center of attention within this physical and spiritual realm, for the spiritual war between Lightness and Darkness has not come to pass yet. Since we are just as much spiritual as well as physical beings, the fate of this spiritual war between God and His rebellious angel, Satan, shall and is an influence in our daily lives. Satan is a defeated foe who has not yet surrendered and received his just punishment. Nevertheless, he still continues to bring havoc and deception upon most of Mankind. Sin is just as much a poison to this Earth as is pollution. Moreover, the violent outburst of Nature is the results of it.

I find it so strange to hear people be quick to blame the Heavenly Father for all of the violence of Nature, especially when it is the free will of humankind to sin and the direct involvement of Satan himself. We are quick to presume that we are not a part of this system or cycle that is called Nature. We would like to believe that we, being the supreme beings, are in fact outside of this cycle; and we try to control and change it. However, in truth, nature is the cycle of life that was created by our Heavenly Father, for He also established a force that is used to keep the cycle of life in balance and to correct any corruption that may endanger it. Mankind has not learned that Father Nature is a system that we as humans must respect and care for. It was not designed for us to conquer and to change, or to control it. To do so would be making a statement that God was in error and that only Mankind can fix the problems of this cycle of life. To learn, to grow, to create, without disturbing that balance of this cycle of life should be the very thing that we embrace and move forward with caution.

It seems to me that sometimes we as humans will spend more time in learning how life is created when we should be learning more of the meaning of life and the byproduct from its' presence. It is good for man to learn about the creation of all things, but it is not enough. To learn the meaning of life is the first step in learning about the creator who created the creation. The Holy Bible is the perfect road map that will help you to discover this truth. What most people do not realize is this: that scientists can only discover and learn about life. They can take life from one thing and life from something else and make something out of it; however, they cannot create life from nothing, nor can they speak life into being. Reality shall someday hit them between the eyes as they learn that God, who is the Father of Christ is

He who is the Father of science, Father of time, Father of nature. He is the Father of all creation and of all things. He is the Father of the Atom and of the DNA strain.

At times, we do seem to forget that since God created us in His image, He would also give us the ability to do things as well: the desire to create; the desire to grow Spiritually, mentally and emotionally as well. He has even given us the ability to become more athletic and so forth. What people don't seem to understand is that God has never stopped being our parent. He is using this world as a play pin or a training ground to teach His Christian children the lessons of life. We cannot learn, grow, and be able to overcome the obstacles in our lives without obstacles in our paths, for Satan is the very obstacle that God is using to help us in our training. Satan is the Mountain that we must climb over. He is the River that we must swim through. Nevertheless, we cannot do it without the help of our God. That is the other part of our training: faith, hope, trust, desires to live a righteous life. He did not make us to be machines or robots. He has given His creation a free will. In addition, for those who have chosen Him, they must receive the training in order to live that spiritual freedom of salvation. To struggle is the process of learning and growing and will help to give some form or shape to our character.

We are living in a time when the world looks at life in a narrow and backward way. They decide in their own way what is right and what is wrong. Their views are not only unlogical but also with no spiritual guidance as well. At times, they will go from one extreme to another and never think twice about it. They have not regard as to what their actions may cause for others, how they could effect the next generation. Common sense and freedom of speech are considered something that would be an offence. They believe that only they can save themselves, as by the will of their own hands. We have even seen this view within Yankee movies. When Mankind is on the verge of coming to an end, secular humanism saves the day! Reality plays just as much a part in creating a fictional story; and the views and values of a writer do bring forth that part of the writer's personality within the story. Once the move has been made, the audience is able to get a small piece of the world from within the writer's mind: a world without moral boundary lines and one in which the responsibilities of one's actions are justified in the eyes of this dying world, a world that would cause an animal species to come close to becoming extinct and put it on the endangered list. Yet this world does not value human life in the same way or even as more valuable. It is all right to eliminate different races, which is the variety of mankind, with the promotion and protecting of abortion and interracial marriage that leads to the destruction of both races. The objective is to destroy the race or races and in every possible way.

Yet it is wrong, in the eyes of the world, to take a race of people and kill them, just as Germany did during World War II. However, homosexuality is protected and promoted to the public, which can lead to a low birth rate and is an abomination in the Eyes of God. It was justified in the eyes of the United State to almost exterminate the Southern people of the Confederacy, including the native Indians of the Confederacy, after the war. I should make this clear to all of y'all: the destruction upon all of the creation of God is not only a sin, but is also a crime against nature. I say that it is a sin because God had put Mankind in charge of caring for the world. Man was not to stand outside of it and abuse it. It is a contradiction to the instructions of the creator. Everything is a testimony to all things of how the verity of all creations, including the verity of the different races of Mankind, points toward our creator. This is the glory and the wonders of life from our God.

One thing is very clear to me, and that is this: Equality within the mind frame of Mankind has no reality or truth to it. The natural realm is the by-product of the spiritual realm, because God is the spiritual creator from this realm, who in fact created the natural realm. Therefore, whatever takes place within the spiritual realm shall also have an effect within the physical realm. Nothing within the physical realm is equal in every way to anything within the physical realm, nor is there anything that is equal in every way within the spiritual realm. I should also point that you should also find nothing that is equal between the spiritual and physical realm either. To say that we are all equal and that we are all the same would be making a direct insult toward our creator, because only in the theory of evolution can everything be equal. To say that a black person is equal to a white person in every way or vice versa is to deny God the credit for all of His creation. To say that a white man is equal to another white man, or black man to a black man, is still making the same statement. Nor are man and woman equal in every way. I must also say that mankind and the animal kingdom are not equal to each other as well. It is true that mankind can still learn a lot about themselves by studying the animal kingdom, for it is a fact that humanity Is part of the chain linked to this cycle of life in which we live.

Governments and religions cannot create and enforce equality within this physical realm. To try to do so is to make an effort to change nature, which would also be an insult toward our God. You cannot find true equality within the theory of Democracy or within the theory of Communism. Moreover, Fascism is nothing more than a theory of oppression and suppression. All three of these forms or theories have to use military force to make these theories into reality. All three of these theories are also a contradiction to the teachings of Jesus Christ. You may ask me what is the true meaning of equality; and my answer would be this:

[In the physical realm]: When in the course of human events, it becomes necessary for one people to dissolve the political bands which have connected them with another, an equal station to which the laws of nature and of natures' God entitle them, a decent respect of the opinions of mankind requires that they:

Should décláré the causes which impel them to the separation. We hold these truths to be self-evident, that all Men are created equal, that they are endowed by their Creator with certain unalienable Rights, that among these are Life, Liberty, and the Pursuit of Happiness. That to secure these Rights, Governments are instituted among Men, deriving their just Powers from the Consent of the Governed. That whenever any Form of Government becomes destructive of these Ends, it is the Right of the People to alter or to abolish it, and to institute new government, laying its Foundation on such Principles, and organizing its Powers in such Forms, as to them shall seem most likely to effect their Safety and Happiness. By: Thomas Jefferson, Of the Declaration of Independence of the United States of America.

It was not just these words that justified the Southern States to leave the Union and form the Federal government of the Confederate States of America. However, it also explains the definition of in what way Men are created equal. The definition of this subject of all men being created equal is based on the natural rights of a free man or a free people, a people that have already earned that natural and basic right that was created by God Himself. Very basic freedoms were not given away, but were earned on the battlefield and are handed down from one generation to the next; freedom that is based upon the moral principles of God and is used as a golden rule for the government of mankind to live by and to protect.; the very freedom that Satan is denying this world. It is a gift by God Himself, for His Creation, and is not nor can be created by any form of government. The Republic of the United States including the Confederate

States of America could only come from the creator who handed down the ideas into the minds of those who wrote the Declaration of Independence as well as both Constitutions of the U.S. and C.S.

Physical slavery is, in itself, not a sin. However it is something that this whole world should not be proud of, for the whole world is guilty of every form of slavery that is established by humankind. Slavery comes in many forms and is not always recognized as such. It is still practiced today, in different ways in the United States of America. I will let you figure out the many forms of slavery within this Yankee Empire. As I have said before, physical slavery is not a sin, for in truth it is a symbol of a world that is living under the spiritual sin of slavery. This physical expression of Mankind cannot see beyond this physical realm; and even within this physical realm, mankind is unable to recognize the warning signs. As it is the Ten Commandments that are the foundation of a moral and a constitutional government of the Republic, it is also true that it is the teachings and the blood of Christ Jesus that break the yoke of bondage that has enslaved Mankind, nor so much within this Physical realm, but within the spiritual realm. People have a hatred for physical slavery; and that is a good and natural emotion, however, people care nothing about the slavery of sin and the spiritual death that will come from it. What can you say about a person who is quick to condemn physical slavery but has rejected the blood of Christ? How much wiser do you think this person is? Not much! – from my point of view.

Our Heavenly Father has used slavery to punish His chosen people for their sinful ways. He has used slavery to lift up His children as well. If slavery were a sin, then He would not have allowed His children to take part in it. Physical slavery has been used by the creator as punishment toward His people, for the next level of punishment would be death. Slavery has been used to teach lessons that He needed His people to learn. It has been through slavery that some slaves have come to hear and accept our Lord Jesus Christ. If someone has chains on his ankles and wrists, yet in spirit has been born again, then he is truly free, while his master is condemned to hell for rejection of our Lord and Savior. Slavery does not always come with chains and whips like you will find in the U.S. propaganda toward the C.S. of A.

Before there were black slaves in the new colonies, they were using white slaves. Africa is just as guilty for enslaving their own race as slaves; and sometimes they would trade the slaves for goods from the slave ships. Slavery has never been just a white man thing or a Confederate thing. Slavery has been a worldly thing long before the birth of Christ. This subject does become very old after awhile, as the United State keeps using it to justify their war crimes toward the Confederate States of America But enough about that.

[In the spiritual realm]: *For God so loved the world that he gave his only Son, So that everyone who believes in him may not perish but have eternal life.* John 3:16. Revised Standard Version, Holy Bible. When it reads *For God so loved the world that he gave his only son*, it was not the world that our Heavenly Father was concerned about; but it was the spirit of mankind that is in this world that He was concerned about. God had sent his son for the mission of Spiritual Salvation and not of physical salvation. The value of a human's life was so high that only the life of Christ could be the ransom. This world tends to put the value of a person's life into different categories of value. People will kill each other for many stupid things and think nothing about it. A person's life can become as cheap as a gold watch or ten dollars in your pocket. Nations will kill each other over natural resources and power, even when there's enough to go around for everybody. People will kill each other because of racial reasons or because of different financial status.

Closing: Mankind has striven to explore this world and the stars up above, yet always fall short in winning the real prize. Mankind has been searching for the fountain of youth while all the while they are decaying from within, always searching to rediscover themselves without looking into the mirror and seeing the final image of the creator that made them. They are much like a dog that is chasing his tail. Once in a while they will finally catch their tail, then realize that they have been running around in circles. Instead of reaching for the stars, they should be reaching out to heaven. Instead of comparing themselves to the animal kingdom, they need to learn who and why God is the way He is.

Instead of striving to grow younger, they should come to accept and follow the footsteps of Christ. The first step in regaining one's youth is to lead a sinless life through Christ. The fate of Mankind is very clear. They will continue to stumble in the daylight with their eyes closed shut until all things take their place in time.

The very foundations of the birth of the Confederacy and those of the Union are, and always have been, the Ten Commandments that God had given to His chosen people. The Ten Commandments are the very fabric that gave strength and structure to both Republics and to the Federal Constitutions. The Ten Commandments have become the Golden Ruler that give principles to one's life and help a society refrain from becoming a beast that preys on itself and others. The Ten Commandments are the guidelines for justice within the courtrooms. Though the Ten Commandments may have been from the Old Testament and are no longer the main commandments for Christian within the New Testament, they are still the umbrella that gives protection to the families of non-Christians. They are also the basic steps in preventing one from sinning, As the Ten Commandments help to prevent one from sinning, it is only the blood Christ that will wash it away.

This is the closest version of the blind leading the blind or the fools who are teaching others to become fools like themselves: The first step in destroying the Republic is not just to strip away the Federal and States' Constitutions, but to also wipe away the Ten Commandments. The reason I say that they must do away with the States' Constitution is because it was the States' Governments that gave power to the Constitutional Republic. Sin has plagued mankind with self-stupidity. The fate of Mankind causes God to step in and intervene for the sake of His creation; but, until that time comes, the struggles will continue between the fools and those that God has given wisdom, especially as to the destiny of this world.

The First Layer

Christianity was the very first layer of the foundation that the Constitutional Republican government of the United States had been founded on. It was the very framework that defines this form of government from every other Nation's government in the world. It was so great by human design that our Confederate Nation had adopted it and made some minor improvements to it. And from that time forward, the Constitutional Republican government of the Confederate States is founded to be the best and superior to any other known government that was designed by mankind. One of the very main purposes of this form of government is to protect and to preserve the Christian beliefs.

It was intended to protect Christianity above any other manmade religion. Catholicism and all other forms of manmade religion have benefited by this protection within the Constitution of the United and Confederate States of America. Even though it was the persecution from the Roman Catholic Church toward Christianity that brought this freedom about in the first place.

The very cornerstone (Christ Jesus) upon which the whole Constitutional Republic is founded is the corner stone that all Nations are to live by. The Old and the New Testament had a great influence in creating these North American governments and rightly so. The influence of the Ten Commandments and the Gospel of Christ became the cornerstone and the framework for these new nations. But some fail to understand that the Ten Commandments were laws for the lawless; and Christ became the law within us that is in Him. The Ten Commandments became the laws without grace and Christ became grace on behalf of the Father. The Ten Commandments are the laws for the mankind of Earth and the Gospel became the laws for mankind of Heaven.

Both are a necessity in order for a Nation to be able to sustain itself and at the same time prosper along the way. Now, I am unable to speak on the behalf of the United State; but here in the Confederate States our heritage and culture are intertwines in both Christ and the Ten Commandments. Part of that culture cleansing is to also remove the teachings of the gospel including the Ten Commandments from our Confederate Americans. Democracy has never cared much for these two subjects. However, it has been known to use them when it comes to political gain; and they are quickly pushed to the side in their law policies. Democracy has learned to use all situations for their person gain. Yet the North American Socialism has no tolerance for anything that is founded in good standing within the Holy Book. They are determined to destroy anything and discredit anyone that is a part of this spiritual awakening. The United States and the Confederate States are the only two true Christian Nations in the whole wide world. Now that the United States has rejected her true foundation, only the Confederacy alone is in good standing as a Christian Nation. Please understand that we do not have our Nation's government here presently to defend our rights since the Federalist Union invasion. And they sure don't care what the Socialist Liberals do in corrupting the minds and the hearts of our children. Nor should we forget that the North American Socialist Liberals and the North American Democracy have been bed partners.

So it's very plain to see that we are on our own, with our only hope being in Christ alone. At this time, our Confederate Nation is slowly slipping away from God, with present foreign heathen religions and idols in our land. The present foreign policies of the United State have rejected the creator. It would seem that we are fighting with one hand tied behind our backs. I have always found it hard to believe how anyone could call himself or herself a Christian and yet support the ideology of socialist American. What the Christian parents don't realize is that they are putting their children in harm's way by allowing their children to become involved in those public indoctrination schools, because those schools are a place for social engineering.

Since 1865, rewritten history has been used to guarantee the loyalty of each generation to the United State. This rewritten history becomes more radical each year; and now these indoctrination camps are also being used as building blocks in our children's character. The teachings of Atheism, Homosexuality, Miscegenation, and other ideas are obtaining a foothold on the minds and the hearts of our children. Once it was the churches that founded and supported the colleges, but that was taken away from them; and now socialism is running amuck in the places of higher learning.

The one thing we have forgotten is this: since the federal governments of the United States and of the Confederate States were founded on the principles of the Ten Commandments and of the Gospel of Christ Jesus, it was therefore intended for these governments to forever remain that way. The freedom of religion that is founded in the Constitution of the Union and of the Confederacy was intended to be for the individuals and not the State or Federal governments. In other words, if you were in office and were not a Christian, you are still required to follow and maintain your office as it was founded, on the *Christian principles of Republican Government*. In fact, it would be best for every State to pass an amendment that makes this clear in their Constitutions. It was never intended by our Founding and Confederate Forefathers to have some other form of Religion to come along and undermine the very concept that Christianity has brought forth in our Governmental institutions. The only purpose for the Freedom of Religion is to protect any person's right and freedom from persecution by anyone of different beliefs.

In fact, both North American Nations should be a safe haven for other Christians of other National origins, instead of allowing every other nonChristian to migrate into our lands. Remember, The Constitutional Rights of the United States and of the Confederate States do not go beyond our National borders. Therefore we have the right to deny citizenship to anyone that is of a heathen religion. Neither the Confederacy nor the Union can be a Nation under God when these Nations have been flooded with other false Gods. One last thing to remember: when in the course of history the Christians become the minority in their own Nation, then they no longer become the voice and the conscience of their Nation; and the judgment of God shall fall upon those Nations that have turned away from Him.

Our Country's Banners

Every flag represents three different things: The first is the identity of someone or something. The second one is the ideas and how those ideas reflect with the relationship with others. The third is the level of authority and sovereignty of each flag. The views on this subject are mine, alone. In addition, I hope that the states of the Confederacy, including our yet to be restored federal government, will consider my point of view on this matter.

1. (The Christian Flag): The Christian flag represents two things. The first is the sovereignty of the most high, who is our creator. The second thing is that the flag also represents a Christian Nation, which is under the teachings of the Son of God. Our laws and society are based on the Gospel of our King. At least they were at one time in our country's history. At any time you fly the Christian banner, you should never fly any other flag above it on the same pole, because nothing is more sovereign than He is. If you have a flag that is a contradiction to the Gospel, then do not have it underneath the Christian flag on the same pole. Whenever you have many flag poles in a line or a circle, never have any other flag flying on the same level and beside the Christian flag. If you have other flags flying on the same level, you are making the statement that those other Countries, etc. have the same amount of sovereignty that God has. It is the way that you fly a flag or flags and the other in which you put them that become a statement that is being made to the public and the rest of the world.

2. (The State Flag): The State flag represents the Country of that State and the sovereignty of that State government. It also represents the authority that the State government has in its State's Constitution and of the membership they have within the constitution of the Confederacy or of the Union. Any State flags of North America should never be flown underneath any National flags of the Confederate States or of the United States. Nor should any National flag be flown at the same level with any State flag. A state that is a member of the Union should never have the present Third National flag of the Confederate States on the same flag pole with the flag of the Union, nor above or underneath that state flag. Nor should any State member of the Confederacy have the present National flag of the United States to be flown on the same flag pole with their State flag, not even above or underneath that state flag. In fact, none of the States of the Confederacy and of the Union should have any other foreign National flag to be present on a flag pole with any other North American State flags. Nor should the National

Banners of either the United States or the Confederate States of America be flown on State government property at any time, for any reason, regardless if the flag is Union or Confederate.

3. (The National Banner): The National banner represents the form of government that is in control at that time in history. The National banner also represents a whole Country or many Countries (States) that have come together in order to increase their protection and security. The National banner should always be flown on federal buildings. It is best not to fly it on public buildings; however, if you do, make sure that it is always underneath your State flag.

At times I have come across Southerners who were flying a Confederate flag with a present Federalist National banner on the same pole or right beside it. These people might be thinking that they love their Country and are, at the same time, proud of their heritage. Unfortunately they do not realize the conflict in that statement. I would ask to explain this more clearly so that everyone will understand this. The invasion of the United States military into the Confederate States' borders had nothing to do with constitutional issues or, as we would call it, the letter of the law. It was about one people that wanted to will their ideas on another people, even with military force. It was also a perfect time to use the hate and fear tactics over the free trade that the Confederacy was putting into place for themselves. Nevertheless, it was necessary to sacrifice the Confederate States of America on the altar on centralism in order to catapult the first phases of Democracy. The Confederacy was the perfect sacrificial lamb at that time in history, because the Confederate States became the very byproduct of those documents that the federalist tyrants wanted to destroy within their own Country.

This was the perfect time to gain power within their own federal government. Above all other reasons to benefit from the war was the cash of the crop. However, military power cannot destroy the truth nor destroy the principles and meaning of liberty that had brought forth this new Nation. Nevertheless, it is most of all by the grace of our God that we have a heritage and culture and a country of our own. The Confederate States of America. This had also become a great opportunity for the industrialists and the abolitionists to join the cause with the federalists and get their pound of Southern flesh. Every National flag of the United States from 1776 to 1860 is a flag that represents the government of the Republic. Every National flag from 1860 to this very present time is a flag of the United State with the (s), known as a form of Democracy. The Confederate people prefer to call these flags of Democracy *Federalist Banners*. Indeed, the National banners of the United States and the federalist banner look almost the same. However, the National flag of the United State has the states of the Confederacy on their banner and a federal government that has committed treason toward the people of the member states of the Union. It is a contradiction to fly any Confederate flag, which fought against that Democracy, and at the same time fly an un-American flag, that wanted to destroy the very ideas of the Republic. These un-American flags would be from the year 1861 to this present time. Some of the Confederate people will fly a flag of the United States, from the period of 1776 to 1860, to pay their respect to the ideas of our Founding Fathers. However, they would never fly that federal banner because they do understand that there is a very big difference between them. Please also remember that our Founding Fathers were both of the Southern and of the Northern States.

The biggest tragedy that our Southern people have not come to understand is this: When they fly a

Federalist banner, this is the statement they are making: "I support the present federal government of the United State; and I condemn the foundation that the United States was founded on. I also deny the fact that we are a separate Country from the United States." Unfortunately, our people have been denied this very truth, for many generations. Moreover, they still believe that we are part of the United States and that everything is the same since the Constitution of the United States and Declaration of Independence were established. Some of our people have lived with this lie for so long that they are unable to handle and cope with the fact that things are not what the Reconstruction camp says they are. However, in order for you to get a better understanding of where I am coming from: Let us say that someone from the Union decided to fly a National Banner of the United States. This person decided to fly the present banner, and this person wanted to fly the banner of 1776. It is this person's idea to celebrate July 4th. The problem with this person's idea is that the banner of the year of 1776 represents a government of the Republic and of the individual States. The present banner represents the centralist federal government and all of the states as being as one unit of one whole. This person is unknowingly making a statement that he is loyal to the original ideas of government and of the identity of the United States. At that very moment, he is also loyal to this present illusionary form of government and Country.

In truth, the 50 stars on the Federalist banner should have been replaced with one large star. In addition, this is including the stars of the Confederate States. However, if they had done this, the people would realize that the federal government was starting to rot from the inside out. Everything must look the same on the outside, in order to give a good appearance, while everything from within was being undone and replaced with something else. It is my personal belief, and that of others as well, that some form of outside invasion from another Country will not destroy the United States of America. The destruction is taking place from within. My view is that it is taking place, at a very slow pace, in order to keep a low profile in the eyes of others. Once the final blow falls upon the people of the Union and of the occupied Confederacy, everything will be ready to set up the New World order or one world government. By that time the people of North America will be at a total loss and fall into the mercy at the feet of this New World government. The people of North America have, for such a long time, been dependent upon the United States of Democracy.

This is what this centralist government had wanted in the first place. In addition, once this centralist government moves into the next level of enlarging itself, the people will have been conditioned to follow the New World government of Democracy. Yesterday the people of the United States were called Yankees. Today they call themselves American citizens. However, tomorrow they may be calling themselves World Citizens or citizens of the world. It is just a question of when and how this change will take place. Nevertheless, it is not written in stone that the United States nor the Confederate States must become members of this New World order. The future is always determined by the Confederate peoples and the Union peoples. It is unfortunate that our Country did not have someone to rescue us from the United States, as had been done on behalf of the country of France during World War II. If it were not for the Alliance of Nations' saving of France, the people of France would be speaking German at this moment and flying the German National banner, including playing the role of good little German citizens. Let us not forget all of those other sovereign Countries that were part of the Russian Empire, who were forced to play the role of the good little Russian.

4. (Battle flag and Navy Jack of the Confederacy): The battle flag of the Confederacy is recognized throughout the world as a symbol of freedom. However, the feelings about this flag are very different within North America today. The present fascist organizations have been using the Confederate battle flag and the National Federalist banner of the United State to promote their racist ideology. Only the battle flag of the Confederacy has been condemned as a symbol of racism. Yet it is the National banner of the United State that has been used, with the support of their government, to commit war crimes and racial strife by military force. I do not find it surprising that the National banner of the United State is not put in the same category as a symbol of racism. Actually the fascist organizations with their own racist views are a blessing and a gift from hell to the socialist left. If I am forced to be politically correct, then I should call them American Communists, since the socialist left has power and influence within the federalist government. They can use these fascist organizations to help them to promote more of their socialist views within our society. I should also point out that some time, not too long ago in our Confederate history, the fascists and socialists had a grand shootout in Greensboro, North Carolina. This took place sometime around the middle of the 1980s. The fascists had won in the Greensboro showdown. However, the socialists were finally able to defeat them in a courtroom. Just to put the record straight, it was the socialists that fired the first shot after the fascists had continually tried to pick a fight with them.

The battle flag or navy flag of the Confederacy was established to be used for the Confederate States' military and navy only. It was not created to be used outside the military, and certainly not for racial or political reasons. Almost every Southerner of race has had a family ancestor who has gone forth to fight and die in order to keep this banner from touching the ground. In addition, no Confederate should ever use these banners, or Celtic or Christian symbols, against any Confederates regardless of race. Laws should be passed by the actual states of the Confederacy to protect all symbols of the Confederacy from being used in a hateful and dishonorable way. Citizens of the states should not be allowed to buy or fly any battle flag or navy jack. If they want to fly their country's flag, then fly the Third National. The battle flag or navy jack should only be used by the military of the Confederate States of America. Moreover, I am talking about the near future. License should be given to only those heritage organizations to use the battle flag for that reason only. Instead of the Confederate civilian population flying the battle flag with our Third National, the proper thing to do is to fly the Bonnie Blue flag instead. The battle flag does not belong on any of the State buildings or on public property. The battle flag is a military banner and should be flown by the military of the Confederate States and of the States' militia.

The battle flag has been used as a symbol of rebellion against society. It is also wrong to use this flag in this sort of manner. The battle flag represents the Republic and just Christianity as much as do our second and third National banners. It is a representation of a society that doesn't need nor want to be in charge nor to have its Republic and Christian way of living replaced with something else that is a contradiction to these ideas or beliefs. This is the reason socialists and federalists have such a hatred for this symbol.

Do you have hatred toward the Confederate or Southern people? Then you would not want to fly or own a flag of the Confederacy. Do you have hatred toward Christianity or the Republic? Then you would not want to fly or own a flag of the Confederacy. Do you have hatred toward other races and cling to the false utopia of segregation? Then you would not want to fly or own a flag of the Confederacy. Do you believe in killing other people for being different or for the self-preservation of your race? Then you would not want to fly or own a flag of the Confederacy, because of the fact that our present Third National flag of the Confederate States of America and the battle flag are symbols of Christianity. In addition, let us not forget about the second National banner. This can only mean that we as a people and as a Nation must carry the teachings of Christ Jesus with us, wherever we go and whatever we do during our times of peace and of war. For if we cannot practice our new life as Christians in the middle of battle toward our enemies, then how can we prove ourselves to those during a time of peace? As a person would tie a string around their finger, in order to remind themselves of something, our Creator made a Rainbow, to remind Him not to flood the world anymore. The Saint Andrew Cross is also a reminder to our people and to our Country of living our personal lives for Him and, in addition, to base the laws of our land, our Country, and our society on Christian principles.

5. (The Bonnie Blue flag): The Bonnie blue flag was the original National Banner for South Carolina at the time that she withdrew her membership from the Union. She was the only state to do so at that very moment in time. After her sister states began to do the same, then the First National Banner became their National flag; and her sister states adopted the Bonnie Blue banner to represent the Banner of Independence. The Bonnie Blue Banner has a history that goes back to the Independence of Texas from Mexico. It is said that the history of the Bonnie Blue could go back as far as the state of Florida. The Bonnie Blue Banner, in truth, is a symbol of a sovereignty of that individual Country that is known as a state. That is why the single star is a representation of Independence for each state. In fact, you might find a single star on some of the State Banners of the Union and of the Confederacy. The Bonnie Blue should always fly below the Christian Banner and above the National Banner. The Bonnie Blue should always fly underneath the State Banner and never below the battle flag. The Bonnie Blue should be flown on top of every State Capitol of the Confederacy underneath the State banner. I also would like to make one statement about the battle flag. It should be flown at the very bottom at all times, regardless of what other Banners are being flown.

The correct way to fly the flags of our Countrymen is in the order below:

1. Christian Banner
2. State Banner
3. Bonnie Blue Banner
4. National Banner
5. Battle Jack Banner

I request that when the Confederate States Congress has been restored that a bill be passed that would accept this *Salute to the Southern Cross* for our present National Banner of the Confederate States of America.

I salute the flag of the Confederate States of America, in memory of the gallant men, women, and children who lived, loved, suffered, and died, fighting for the right to be free. Under God, with affection, reverence, and undying devotion to the cause for which it stands.

It is very important for everyone to understand that at no time should we put our hands over our hearts and pledge our allegiance to anything or anyone else. To pledge your allegiance to something means that your loyalty does not belong to anything or anyone else. Not even to God the Father and His Son. When we accepted Jesus Christ as our personal saver, we made devotion to Him a pledge of Allegiance to the Son, Christ, and to no other. To live our life for Him and His Father, before and above anything else. It is one thing to pay our respect by saluting the banner of our State and Nation. However, it is a whole different story for us to pledge our loyalty to something. If you are a citizen of one of the states, in which you live, and that state was a member of the Confederacy or of the Union, then your obligation to defend your state and Nation becomes a natural right and responsibility as a patriot. It is not necessary for you to continually remind yourself and the Federal government of your responsibilities. It is just possible that the Federalist government is indeed afraid of a rebellion from the states. By having the people to continually repeat this pledge of allegiance, it uses a form of self-brainwashing and conditioning. In fact, our children are being forced to learn this early in public schools. If, in fact and in truth, we are Confederates and some of us are Christians, then this pledge of allegiance is a mockery and an insult to all that we stand for and believe in. If, at any time, there is a conflict between your loyalty to your state government and your federal government, then you should begin to question the possibility of treason afoot. The Republic was designed to work in a form that would make sure that no one would violate the amount of authority of power, so that the state government and the federal government could run together in harmony and without conflict.

8 of December 2001
John T. Nall

Taxation Without Representation

Luke 20:22-25 (The New Revised Standard Version):

Is it lawful for us to pay taxes to the emperor or not? [23] But he perceived their craftiness and said to them. [24] "Show me a denarius. Whose head and title does it bear?" They said, "The emperor's". [25] He said to them, "Then give to the emperor the things that are the emperor's and to God the things that are God's."

In what way does this apply to us? Should we pay taxes, and is this a contradiction to the ideas of our Founding Fathers? These are good questions, and the answers to them are very simple. Let me begin by saying: Our nation of the Confederacy is under the same situation with the Yankee Empire as the Nation of Israel was with the Roman Empire. We are submitting to and under the protection of the Yankee Empire just as the Nation of Israel was with the Romans. We carry money in our possession that has the name of that foreign government, with the pictures of the presidents who were in office at the time, just as Israel carried Roman money. As long as our Confederate people are under the rulership of the government of the United States, we must abide by their rules. We must pay taxes to the Yankee Empire and do as they say, up to a point. However, to submit to compromising our Christianity and to submit to any form of genocide is non-negotiable. Once we have been delivered from their occupation, with the mercy and grace of our creator, then all forms of taxes must come to a complete stop.

If this is true, then what about the States who are members within the Union? Should they pay taxes? I say "No". The Constitution of the United States does not allow taxation without Representation. The only taxes that are legal would be on the products that you buy and on imports and exports. The situation does not fall under the same category of the subject of which Christ was speaking. All of these taxes are used in one way or another to build and support that Empire that is in fact a damnation to the principles and ideas of the Constitution of The United States, including the Constitution of our Confederate States. This is a problem that member states of the Union need to deal with.

Some people have come to believe that paying taxes is a business transaction. They believe that they are supposed to receive something in return. Nevertheless, this is not always the case. There are two forms of taxes. The first is a tax that people vote for to accomplish a certain goal. If you are a County or State, having requested a tax from the people to improve the roads or for the schools, then the tax falls into the hands of the people. The other form of tax is forced upon the people without their consent. You are expected to shut up and pay this tax. You do not know, in this case, where your tax dollars are going, nor do you have a say about how much the tax shall be. If you do not pay these taxes, everything that belongs to you can be taken away. You might even be imprisoned for failure to pay. This is the meaning of "Taxation without Representation".

Whose Foreign Policy Is It Anyway?

Like it or not, our people and our Confederate Nation shall reap the outcome of the foreign policies of the Yankee Empire, regardless of what that may be. As long as we are under their jurisdiction, whatever fate shall come to them shall Be our fate as well. The form and actions of any foreign policies can bring the problems directly to the doorsteps of the people of that Nation and to the Nations that they occupy. The policies could cause a *Nose that was slammed in the Door* effect/ordeal, meaning that the problems of the world could pull us into the middle. The kind of policies that would cause such a situation: world wars, the outcome of the 11 of September 2001 (the fruit that came from the garden of the Yankee Empire's foreign affairs). The greatest tragedy is not the number of deaths that happen during the course of these foreign affairs, for death is a natural process of life; but the tragedy is not questioning why these deaths have taken place and not holding that Federal government accountable for their participation in the whole matter.

Indeed, when the citizens start to add up as a death count, then by all rights justice should be given not only to those who pulled the trigger, but also to anyone who caused that someone to pull that trigger. I have seen how quickly my people allow emotional tragedy to overcome all logical and reasonable questions and concerns of their judgment. Even when it comes to the loyalty toward the Yankee Empire, my Confederate people have always been a loyal and caring kind of people and I believe that when it comes to being patriotic, my people hold this meaning closer to their hearts than anyone else. This is even true when their patriotism is misguided at times. The reality is this: if the terrorist attacks had taken place toward a Southern state and were directed toward our people, then by all means the majority of the Yankee National would not fly Confederate flags on their cars and buildings. You might even find a small amount of them that would even care enough to cry for our lost.

Despite how much our people try to be good little Yankees, the Yankees have always considered us to be something that they must tolerate. But enough with the comparisons between the two. When it comes to the actions of any State or Federal governments, questions should always be asked; and the actions and decisions should always be accounted for., always to the people themselves, alone. Here are some questions to think about.

1. Is the foreign policy of the United State that of a Republic or of a Democracy?
2. If it were a foreign policy based on a Republic, then wouldn't it be regulated by the constitution of that Nation?
3. Wouldn't it be controlled in some way and kept in check?
4. If so, then how is it kept in check?

5. Has any Nation committed an act of aggression that would cause the sovereignty of the States and Federal government to be in danger?
6. And in return cause the federal government to make a declaration of war?
7. Has the federal government been using other people in foreign lands as puppets to control these foreign governments?
8. Has the federal government ever used criminals to do their dirty work?
9. Have they ever murdered anyone in the name of National Security?
10. Has this government ever committed any war crimes or violated anyone's human rights for any reason?
11. If so, then when, where, and why, and how many times?
12. Has information on any subject been misused and controlled to influence the people in order to gain support for war and invasions?
13. Do the people truly know everything that their federal government is doing within these foreign lands?
14. Has the Federal government done anything in these foreign lands that would cause a backlash or war

The thing that everyone keeps overlooking is this: We have had many different forms of terrorism in North America. We have had the great John Brown and his thugs of abolitionists, war crimes by the military of the United States toward the citizens of the Confederacy, race rots in the cities and towns, the aggression of fear and violence toward the southern Negroes by the Ku Klux Klan, the aggression from the civil or socialist rights movement in order to agitate the southern Caucasian citizens into violence for the TV broadcasting stations, and the using of military muscle by the federal government in order to force social engineering upon the citizens as well as violation of the will of the majority of the people's voice. But terrorism from outside the North American continent are something that is a very different matter.

The terrorist attacks on the 11 of September 2001 are not what I believe to be as it is promoted on the news and by the federal government. I do not believe that it was an act to destroy our so-called freedom, nor do I believe that it was directed toward our Christianity or faith. The act of violence was directed toward specific targets and is not a random act toward everybody. It was not directed toward the churches and towns and places of common people. It was not something that takes place every day. The act of violence was directed toward the Pentagon and toward the White House. It was directed toward the world trade center as well. This act of terror was directed toward the foreign policies of the government of the United State and of the United Nations; and it should be clear so that we remember this fact. It is true that Christians are and always will be persecuted in other foreign lands, and it has always been this way; but we should remember that the United State government no longer represents the moral practices of a Christian government and Nation. It is also clear that the world trade center and the One World Bank, including the United Nations, are working together to enslave us more into the New World Order or One World government. The sad fact in all of this is that the people who were not involved in this conflict paid the price in the outcome of this action. It saddens my heart to say this, but like sheep to the slaughter house, the people will allow this tragedy to repeat itself over and over again. As long as they ignore the signals of a dying Nation and rotten fruit it bears, a greater form of slavery shall not end.

God bless America is a statement that you will find on bumper stickers, etc.; but does it have any true meaning at all? First, the statement is not clear at all, for it is making a plea for God's blessing for the continents of all America. We all know, however, that the meaning is meant to be directed toward the United State of America. The correct statement should be *God bless the United State of America*; but would this still have a true meaning. The answer would be "no". A Nation is not blessed just for the fact that it is a Nation, nor for the fact that this Nation would be blessed above all other Nations. Nations will come and go, and God has no concern about this most of the time, unless this Nation is taking part in His plans. The only blessing that is given to a Nation is that given to His children of Christ of the New Testament and of the faithful ones in the Old Testament. God has no concern for those who are against him and have rejected his son. A Nation can only benefit from the blessings that he has given to his children and it is for this reason only that this Nation shall prosper. Ask yourself this? What the United State as Nation done to deserve to be blessed by God? And what changes need to be made to receive his blessings?

If you have never heard of our constitutional Anthem of *God Save The South*, then by all means, you need to hear it. It is a beautiful piece of work and music. It will fill your heart with pride and self-respect for our people and Nation; but even the title of our National Anthem is a statement that we should touch on a little. In order for God to save the south, he will have to do so by his grace, and his grace alone. It will not be by the power of our hands and our rich and beautiful heritage. Obedience to him will give him the desire to be concerned with everything that we do, even when it comes to the sovereignty of our State and Nation. At all times, and in every aspect, to humble ourselves to him and give all glory to him for all things during the good and bad times. To do all of these things and to remember all of these things shall once more become the very freedom for our people and Nation.

Race Relations In Dixie

In times of our Confederate history, our race relations with each other here in the land of Dixie have been like a roller coaster. It is a natural thing to find strife between two or more races; but this is something that you will find anywhere in the world. In fact, if you only had one race, without the influence of another outside race, you would still find conflict within that one race. The two greatest frictions that have caused more racial hatred between the races in the Confederacy are Satan and the government of the United State. Satan thrives on the emotions of people in order to play them like fools. It gives him pleasure to destroy the lives of people. The United State government has worked hard to keep a barrier between the white and black race, in order to keep them from coming together as a Nation, for if this were to happen, the South would indeed rise again as a Nation.

In reality it was the Yankee Nation's invasion that brought all Southern Confederates of every race to stand together in order to defend their home, country and Nation. After the invasion, it was that same Yankee Nation that brought havoc and hell on earth and established a division and power struggle between the races, a power struggle as to who would become second and third class citizens of the occupied states of the Confederacy within the Yankee Empire. Ever since the aftermath of the present occupation of the Yankee Empire, the United State government has been using the Confederate Negroes (including the Union Negroes) as puppets for their political games and power. Hatred and fear are great and powerful weapons used to control and to keep the Confederate States under submission and strife. Being deprived of our sovereign identity as Confederates and of knowing and understanding our Southern or Confederate Heritage and culture, a vacuum took place that allowed other influences to creep into our society in Dixie.

Facism was directed toward the white population, while Communism was directed toward the black population. One thing is very clear to me: that politics will use the racial card in order to gain control or power over a Nation, if that is what it takes. The aftermath of the white power parties has the philosophy of fascism, while communism gave birth to the social rights or civil rights movement in North America. In truth, the Confederate people have never been given the time to heal themselves and deal with the problems at hand without outside interference from the Yankee Empire. The White southerners and the Black southerners, including other southerners of race, do share the same heritage and culture. Almost all of us eat the same kind of food (Soul Food); and we, as a Nation, are founded on the gospel of Christ. We have a history with each other of good and of bad times; and in truth, we do not need the ideology of communism and its' social engineering, nor do we need the fascism and its' inferior ideology of stupidity. Nor do we need the present monster (Yankee Empire) that is pouring the poison of democracy into our Confederate land.

It is imperative that the White Confederate Americans relearn and understand that the Black Confederate Americans need to be treated as equal citizens under both constitutions of the state and Confederate governments, that no one should be treated as first, second, nor third class citizens because of the color of their skin. It was the ancestors of these Black Confederate Americans who fought, died, and suffered in defense of Dixie in the cities and out in the fields. They have not only earned the right to their place in our history, but also the right to stay here and to become citizens within the states of the Confederacy. They have earned that right to liberty and to be treated as equals under the constitutions of both the State and federal governments of the Confederacy, for if it had not been for them, the war would have ended far sooner than it did. The native Confederate Indians should also be given citizenship for the contributions of their ancestors of the southern cause. Equality should be on the basis of the teachings of Jesus Christ and be restored into our southern society. If one person of color becomes a Christian, and that person meets another Christian person of another race, they both become as one family in the spirit, but not in the flesh; and they must treat each other as one family in the spirit of Christ.

The only thing that we need to heal our racial struggle is the gospel of Christ within our society, our culture, and southern heritage. Let us not forget the peaceful removal of the United State from our Confederate soil. Whenever you have two or more races that are living among each other, it is necessary to have a good balance between segregation and integration. The down side to this is that whenever you are enforcing one (alone) of the two, it becomes self-destructive for both races. Segregation alone can cause the other race to be treated as second-class citizens and, even worse, less human. Integration alone will cause the end result of miscegenation and will cause both races to be on the endangered list. By the same token, the wealthy and the poor have also treated each other as first and second-class persons. It is clear that we as human beings can learn a lot of good and bad things from other races. In truth, it is a blessing and a curse to have an integrated society.

We must come to learn and respect the right of self-preservation as long as it does not violate the self-preservation and constitutional rights of anyone else. It is not a constitutional right for anyone that desires to do harm, to their own race or to another race. Nor should Governments of State or federal entities take part in enforcing the laws of integration and segregation upon their citizens. The constitutions were written for all who are of citizenship, and not based on the wealth of a person nor the color of their skin, nor one's sexual gender. The constitutions of the State and of federal government are documents of morality just as much as they are of rights and limited powers of government. Therefore a citizen cannot be protected under any constitution during the course of active immorality. A simple course of observation of the Confederate Negroes is not to cause harm to them. In fact, it is quite the opposite. I do not believe in removing the Negroid race from the States of North America any more than I believe in putting them to death. But from my observation, It appears to me that they promote the rights as a Black race while committing self-racial genocide. They are either filled with envy of the white race or have hatred toward them. They are allowing Satan to play and to control their emotions, and, at the same time, they have allowed the politicians of both the black and the white race to play them for fools and puppets for centuries. When they are name-calling someone else as a racist, it is surely they that are racist against their own race. They must overcome this selfpity and stop blaming the environment that they live in and the white race for their shortcomings. instead, they must put their trust in God for help and guidance and learn to face and overcome the difficult times that life will bring. Whenever injustice falls upon them, it is important that they stand up and proclaim their rights as citizens and not as a race. For when they used the issue of race they automatically separate themselves from all other citizens. As civil rights or socialist rights are unconstitutional, they must stand on the rights of their state and federal constitutions. To be treated equally under the constitution is not, nor can it ever be, to treat one group in a special way. The white race has been guilty of doing this for years, when they have treated the Negroid race as second-class citizens. Two wrongs don't make a right. All must be given the same opportunity and choices in life, then deciding what their capabilities may be. After all, we are all not the same in every way.

The Confederate States and the United State have never been a one race society and Nation. Each group has its values and contributions just as each one is a part of the body when it is working together for the goodness of all. However, a mongrel and a multicultural people and Nation could never be an improvement for us all. Instead it will only put the final nail into our coffin as a People and as a Nation.

Slavery

I want to cover some areas about the subject of slavery about which you may never have heard. Slavery has built nations and empires. Every race and both sexes have been guilty of voluntary and involuntary servitude. Slavery was and is still a way of life in some parts of the world; and slavery comes in many forms. An individual could be a slave and not realize it! In fact, a nation "meaning the people" could be enslaved and not have the realization of this fact.

People could be enslaved by the teaching of propaganda, by withholding truthful information regarding history, and the lack of knowledge of their country's government, how it functions and what form of government they were meant to have.

Empires have dominated a country or more than one country, using the slaves of these countries to fight their enemies. They have forced and will force these dominated countries to be loyal to their governmental empire in that country.

Through ignorance, most of these slaves believe in their own hearts and minds that they are true members of the empire; and at times, their loyalty is not to the truth, but to the power and wealth that they can gain from it. Those who seek freedom from tyranny shall fall victims to these scalawags, who have no honor and value in truth and liberty.

The best definition of Old Testament slavery is what we would call "a quick fix". (1) It's a quick way to increase economical needs of the country.

(2) It's a great way to cause a country to grow bigger and stronger within a short amount of time. (3) It helps one country to be able to compete with other countries who may or may have slaves. Slavery was, and is still, a way of life. Even though the institution of slavery has changed in some nations, it is still, nonetheless, a part of our lives.

I'm sure that you've heard the typical Yankee lies or propaganda that "slavery is a sin"! The truth is that slavery is not a sin; however, slavery can lead the slaveowner into sin. This is why God had to step in and to give guidelines within the institution itself. I personally do not believe in the institution, nor do I desire to have any slaves under my care. It is hard enough to deal with my own salvation as I'm walking in the path of Jesus Christ without having to worry about the salvation of those under my care. I know that on the day of judgment, I would have to answer to my God when it comes to the condition and treatment of the slaves that might have been under my care.

The institution of slavery can cause great side effects, that could affect our society and the country as a whole and it can create a gateway that Satan can use to bring about sin and cruelty.

Laws were in place to protect the slaves from mistreatment within the slave states of the Union, but there were no guarantees that crimes would be reported or that the suspects would be found – much like the laws that we have today. So let me wipe away that mystical cloud that has fogged up your mind: "Yankee propaganda" and help face some facts about that so-called "Land of the Free".

Fact Number One: Slavery was protected within the Constitution of the United States, all of the way up to the invasion into the Confederacy. Fact Number Two: Slavery was repealed from the U.S. Constitution two years after the war had ended between the United States and the

Confederate States.

Fact Number Three: If the Southern States wanted to keep slavery alive and to promote the institution in the near future they would never have left the Union!

Fact Number Four: Once they left the Union, the institution of slavery within the Southern States would no longer be protected under the U.S. Constitution.

Fact Number Five: Because of the withdrawal of the Southern States from the compact of the Union of States if a slave were to break free, go on the run, and escape from that slave state into a Union non-slave state, then that slave could not be forced back to the slaveowner within the slave state.

Fact Number Six: When the Southern States were within the Union, the runaway slave had to be sent back to the owner.

Fact Number Seven: Once the Southern States left the Union, they lost all rights and the power to cast a vote within the Yankee government, meaning that neither the Confederate States' government nor the membership of those Southern States could have stopped the U.S. government from repealing the slave law from the Constitution of the United States.

Fact Number Eight: And so, whether or not the Confederacy was forced back into the Union and whether or not the Union had invaded the Confederacy, the leaders within the Northern States could have done away with slavery at any time. So the next time someone says that the United States fought to free the slaves, be sure to inform that person that this is nothing more than a Yankee lie!

Fact Number Nine: The Constitution of the Confederate States would have slowly caused the institution of slavery to phase out. This would have given this new nation extended time to heal itself from this practice and to find something better to replace it. This is what all of the slave countries have done over the years, as well as the Northern States.

Fact Number Ten: The Northern States had benefitted greatly in so many ways from the institution of slavery the importation of slaves from the Yankee slave ships and the shipment of goods and products from the Southern States into the Northern States.

Fact Number Eleven: The government of the United States had passed a law that would stop the importation of slaves into the states, but either they did not enforce it or they did not try hard enough. As far as I know, there was no law to stop the slaves from being bought, once they came to shore.

Fact Number Twelve: Conclusion: The Southern States did not leave the Union because of the slavery issue. It did play a small part in the outcome.

Fact Number Thirteen: It was intended that the Federal Government should provide a balance of power and protect the needs of all of the states within this Union, which also meant to keep one or more states from having control over any other states within that government. The representatives of each state were based on the population. This was meant to help each state avoid being always outvoted.

Have you ever wondered why the leaders of the Southern States wanted to increase slavery in the western areas. Yes, it was the Northern States who did not want to do so. Slavery was not a moral issue to the South because slavery is not a sin in the eyes of God. However, it was an issue of having a political voice in Congress. Some people felt that slavery was evil and that the western slavery was a bad idea.

In my view, the population of the Northern States was growing day by day, and yet the population of the Southern States basically stayed the same. The biggest reason for this is that not everyone would want to be a farmer. With the increase of the population in the north was an increase of representatives; and so, had the western states become slave states, this might have evened the voting power within the House. It is also true that some Northern leaders did not want a balance of power within the House, because they might lose control over the government.

The 3/5ths Rule from Article 1 of the U.S. Constitution (Library of Congress), In order to compromise the issue of taxation and representation of slavery with the Northern/Southern States, the 3/5ths Compromise was issued in Article 1 Of the U.S. Constitution. In the compromise, black slaves counted 3/5ths of an American citizen in terms of political representation and taxation.

Article 1 of Section 2 of Paragraph 4 within the original 7 Articles of the U.S. Constitution reads Representatives and direct taxes shall be apportioned among the several states which may be included within this Union, according to their respective numbers, which shall be determined by adding to the whole number of free persons, including those bound to service for a term of years, and excluding Indians not taxed, three-fifths of all other persons.

(Holy Bible)

John 8: 31 – 38

[31] Then Jesus said to the Jews who had believed in him, "If you continue in my word, you are truly my disciples;
[32] And you will know the truth, and the truth will make you free."
[33] They answered him, "We are descendants of Abraham and have never been slaves to anyone. What do you mean by saying, 'You will be made free?'"
[34] Jesus answered them, "Very truly, I tell you, everyone who commits sin is a slave to sin.
[35] The slave does not have a permanent place in the household; the son has a place there forever.
[36] So if the Son makes you free, you will be free indeed.
[37] I know that you are descendants of Abraham; yet you look for an opportunity to kill me, because there is no place in you for my word.
[38] I declare what I have seen in the Father's presence; as for you, you should do what you have heard from the Father."
[39] (The New Revised Standard Version)

Comment:

Our Messiah's words are clear. If slavery was a sin within the physical realm, then He would have made a statement about it within this subject. However, it was in his view and the view of the Father that sin is indeed the reality of slavery within the Spiritual realm. Nevertheless, as you may learn in the teachings of Jesus Christ, it is not just accepting Him as your saver that is important. It is also important to treat others as He wants you to treat them as well. If you were to treat other differently from the way He commanded, then this would also be a sin. I request that you study this further.

The Western States

Each Western State is a unique country. Each has a unique heritage and culture that you won't find in the rest of the States of the Union. They have a very colorful history that has become the ideal dream of North America. That dream is "Having plenty of elbow room without anybody yanking your chain". They are a peaceful people that mind their own affairs and only care about taking care of their family and town folks. Yet, their heritage and culture are just as much in danger as is our Confederate heritage. It would be impossible for the Western States to fit into this coming Third World society of a one-world government. Therefore the destruction of their Heritage and Culture must take place in order for them to fit into this warped dream of utopia. This is the same reason that our Confederacy is under attack to this very day. The only people who are able to save these Western States is those that live there. However they are unable to do it without the help of our Heavenly Father. The first step that needs to be taken is this: They must pray to God and ask Him to restore their government of the Republic and to restore and to protect their Heritage. They should also pray and ask God if He wants their States to withdraw their membership from the Union. The next thing they need to do is to pray for our Confederate States of America. Most of all, we need to be praying for them and trying to help them when it is necessary!

A time will come when the Western States will be pushed against the wall. It is very important that they be cautious in taking the next step at that time. I will lay out a game plan for them to use. If the first step does not work, then they should move on to the next step and so forth.

1. Work to restore the government of the Republic, within the United States. If this fails, then take the next step.
2. "Secession" – If they withdraw from the Union too soon, the Yankee Empire might use their military bases within the occupied Confederacy and force the Western States back into the Union. This is why they should try Step 1 first.
3. If secession becomes necessary, they can create their own federal government for the Western States only. If they do not take this route, I can only hope that they will establish good relationships with our Confederacy.
4. If they should desire to join our Confederate States of America, they will not be able to do so until our Federal government of the Confederate States has been restored and the Union military bases are removed from our Southern borders. I want to make it clear that the destruction toward the Southern States will fall upon the Western States as well, if it has not started already.

The Western States of the Union and Southern States of the Confederacy do, in fact, have a lot in common. Therefore I believe that we should strive to have a strong friendship with the West. We should pray for them and stand by their side, no matter what path these Western States may take in order to protect the future and safety of their people. The Western States could learn a lot from our Confederate history. To do so would give them a better stronghold for the future and liberty. Let us pray that they will learn these lessons of life. The State governments must relearn the lesson that has been lost with the unconstitutional war of the Union upon our Confederacy. That lesson is this: For as long as that State government does not violate their State and Federal Constitution in order to represent and protect the citizens of their State, they shall continually stand up and bring the dream of liberty into reality. However, they cannot do so for as long as they are under the submission of slavery to the unconstitutional rulership of the Federal government. For far too long the State governments have found themselves between the rock and a hard place.

If it should come down to secession, the Western States should wait four to five years before seceding. First they must build their military and expect the invasion by the United States. They might receive some Confederate who might desire to come and join in their defense. Nevertheless they should not rely on the Confederacy as a Nation, due to the present occupation of that foreign federal government and their troops. Whatever path the Western States should take, they should do so with caution. Self-preservation is a natural form of defense for every living thing. Self-preservation comes naturally for a person and a people and a Country.

Self-preservation is a very good and important thing. However it is important to understand that Satan will use every possibility to trap his victims, in order to use the emotions of the people against them. Hatred and envy are the two greatest weapons of sin that he has in his arsenal. Hatred and envy are also the fundamental weapons of the socialist movement of communism in North America. It is a way to create a division between the differences of the people, moving toward a collision and establishing the outcome of equality in the socialist form.

It is clear that as long as these Western States continue to stay within this centralized Union of democracy, their fate is doom. If they desire, they can hold out and wait for the collapse of the Yankee Empire and start over once more. In fact, this is exactly what the Confederate States are trying to do. I understand that it would be hard for them to leave the Union. I can only hope that they will be able to solve these problems in a better way than our beloved southland. Nevertheless, if it does come to that point, they should understand that this is just part of the growing pains of liberty. It is always difficult to leave something that you have been a part of. It was hard for the British colonies to leave the British Empire, but it became necessary for them to do so. It was hard for the Southern States to leave the Union. Nevertheless it became necessary. The same may some day be true for the States of the West. Only God knows what their future holds.

Preserving Their Resources

Every Empire or super world power is like a giant Octopus. It will naturally have its tentacles stretch out upon the nations that are under its dictatorship. Like all Empires, the more it grows, the weaker it becomes. In time it could become difficult to guard its Grande borders in defense; and it could become very expensive. The Confederacy would be able to relieve the Yankee Empire from some of this burden, but we must be able to convince them in a way that will give them the desire to remove their Yankee forces from our Sovereign State of our Confederacy. It is clear, in history, that our Confederate Nation would fight over constitutional principles. It is also clear in history that the Federalist Union will fight over economical issues. Therefore it becomes the responsibility of us Southrons to try to arrange a deal that will make them feel safe when it comes to the trade issues, an arrangement that will make them feel that they could benefit more by freeing our Nation from their grasp. We have a few ideas that we could share with them, so let's make a deal!

1. In allowing those States governments, which were going to vote on the issue of secession, but were overthrown by Federal troops, to be allowed to finish the debate over secession and to allow those State to vote on that issue.
2. To establish an equal trade system with the Federals without causing harm to the economy of both Nations, by making them partners and hopefully establishing a free trade with the rest of the world.
3. That the federals will no longer be guarding the Confederate borders that are between the Confederacy and the Nations of Mexico and Canada.
4. That the Federals will no longer be responsible in for guarding the Confederate shorelines.
5. No longer having the Federals spend federal aid and FEMA in the occupied Confederacy.
6. No longer having the Federals share government powers with the States of the South.

The federalist Jacobins would benefit greatly in this way. They would be able to save more time and resources including the extra manpower which could be used in other areas of their Empire. A peace treaty must be established between the U.S. of A. and the C.S. of A.. In this treaty it must be clear that the Union or Federalist Nation shall never again establish a shoreline blockade against the Confederacy and never again send military forces into the Confederate States without the permission of the Confederate government unless, of course, in the case of other foreign powers that were to invade our beloved Confederacy. The treaty must make provisions for the use of Confederate forces, in the event of an invasion into the United State by any foreign Nation, to protect the States governments and Capitols of their former Republics.

I am not saying that we should compromise our views and principles with any evil Empire. Nor should we condone the actions of the former Republic of the United States, because it is clear that in history all Empires await its fate. Perhaps, if we can avoid being pulled down with them, maybe we can be able to protect them and stand by their side, providing they desire to restore their constitutional Republic of the United States in the near future. However, if they should desire to establish some other form of government, or if they should break into other small Nations, then it is not our place nor responsibility to interfere. Our only responsibility is to honor and to protect the memory and the ideology of our founding Forefathers, who originally established the United States of America. One thing is clear, those that are the enemies of the United State see us as their enemies also, because the world does not know nor understand that we are a separate Nation, apart from the former United State of America. It is also clear that our Confederate people are still spellbound by the unconsciousness that had fallen upon the mythical personages of Sleeping Beauty and Snow White. Until the time that we awake, we are unable to protect ourselves from the predator within the woods.

Black Powder

Article 1 of Section 9, Number 13, of the Constitution of The Confederate States says this: "A well-regulated militia being necessary of a free State, the right of the people to keep and bear arms shall not be infringed". You'll also find that in the Article VII, Amendment 2, of the Constitution of The United States that says: "A well-regulated militia, being necessary to the security of a free state, the right of the people to keep and bear arms shall not be infringed". If we were to look at this more closely, we would see that this "right" is of two parts in one whole statement. This first part is talking about the ability of a sovereign state to defend itself and its States Constitution by using a militia in order to remain independent and free. And to remain a free or sovereign state is to deny anyone from ruling over them, regardless of the relationship with the Federal government of member states that has become corrupted, or from any other unwelcome foreign invasion. For if the State is unable to defend the powers and the liberties of its citizens within their Constitution, then that state is no longer free. Since the states of the old United and Confederate States no longer have this basic right, then this can only mean that we aren't any longer a free people.

The second part of this statement is talking about the people themselves. To infringe is to control or to regulate or to do away with. Therefore, to do this is the very violation upon the rights of the people themselves. The Federal government does not have the legal right to say what kind of weapon or the amount of ammo a person cannot have. Nor can they deny a person the right to bear a weapon on their persons. Nor does it say rather or not in what way it is not legal to have that weapon on them. The reason for this is because it is the people who in times of emergency shall become the militia during war or civil strife.

But it also covers the basic right of the people to protect themselves and loved ones, for the protection of their personal property, and also for the purpose of hunting for food. We can honestly say that this would not apply to those who have committed a violent criminal act or who have a mental record, to maintain that right. However, the citizens who haven't violated the trust of the people of that state and the responsibility of the liberties that go along with it should never be violated. I should also make it clear that the Federal Constitution did not originally come into conflict with the State Constitution; therefore it prevents the State and the Federal governments from violating each other's Constitutions. The federal Constitutions are, in fact, additional or extra rights that the State has as a free member in the Union or Confederation.

The last line of defense is the people themselves, from those who live in the big cities to the folks that may live in the small towns and the back woods. To deny this right is to make the statement that we are not to be trusted or that those who are violating our true freedom have become fearful of us. To remain free is to be responsible to not abuse those privileges. Because anything can be used as a weapon, even if guns were to be denied to the people, it is the people who are the master over their actions and not the objects that they use to commit the crimes.

In Article 1 of Section 9 of the Constitution of The United States is stated the right to raise and support armies, but *no appropriation of money for that use shall be for a longer term than two years.* (Comments: In other words, not to continually maintain an army)

To provide and maintain a navy. (Comments: This means that all other military forces other than the navy that are continually maintained during peaceful times are in violation of their Constitution and is therefore illegal)

To make rules for the government and regulation of the land and naval forces.

To provide for calling forth the militia to execute the laws of the Union, suppress insurrections, and repel invasions. (Comments: This means that all other military forces other than the navy that are continually maintained during peaceful times are in violation of their Constitution and is therefore illegal)

To make rules for the government and regulation of the land and naval forces.

To provide for calling forth the militia to execute the laws of the Union, suppress insurrections, and repel invasions. (Comments: The insurrection is the intent of the people or of the States that have started a revolution to overthrow the Constitutional Republic government of The United States.)

To provide for organizing, arming, and disciplining the militia, and for governing such part of them as may be employed in the service of the United States, reserving to the states respectively the appointment of the officers and the authority of training the militia according to the discipline prescribed by Congress. (Comments: This part is talking about using a portion of the militia from each State, under the Command of the United States and respecting each State's right to use the remains of the militia in defense of that State.)

Further down from this you will see:

To make all laws which shall be necessary and proper for carrying into execution the foregoing powers. And all other powers vested by this Constitution in the government of the United States, or in any department or officer thereof. (Comments: This is sometimes called the "elastic clause" because it can be interpreted to give many powers not actually mentioned in the Constitution. In other words, The Federalist believes that the Constitution is void because they are above the limitations of the authority that the Constitution allows the Federal government to have. A simple way to put it is a "government of Democracy".)

In Section 9, you'll find *the privilege of the writ of habeas corpus shall not be suspended, unless when in cases of rebellion or invasion the public safety may require it.* (Comments: "Habeas corpus" guards against unjust imprisonment by requiring a judge or court to decide whether a person may be held. Yet this does not give the government the power to violate the freedom of speech. Nor does it give them the power in shutting down or controlling the Presses. Nor does it give them the power to imprison someone during a war and never bring him or her to trail at the end of the war. To do these things would violate the rights of that person. And it would also be making a statement that the freedom of speech to disagree with the government becomes an act of rebellion. Thus, the individual rights become an act of violation.

In Section 2 is stated regarding the Powers of the President that *the*

President shall be Commander in Chief of the Army and Navy of the United States, and of the militia of the several Sates, when called into the actual service of the United States; he may required the opinion, in writing, of the principal officer in each of the executive departments upon any subject relating to the duties of their respective offices, and he shall have power to grant reprieves and pardons for offences against the United States except in cases of impeachment. (Comments: The president does not have the power to use the military forces in any way without Congress making a declaration of war. Nor does it say anything about him having powers over the Air Force. It is clear that to some point the Constitution needs to be updated; however, if it were being ignored, then what would be the point?

The Constitution of the Confederate States is a remake and an improved version of the Constitution of the United States. The comments I've made concerning the Union Constitution also apply to the Confederate Constitution. The most important thing for the military forces to remember is that they are entrusted by the people, to protect the citizens from hostile Nations and to protect the Constitution of their Federal government as it is written. When the military acts on the whim of the Federal government and ignores that duty to preserve the true government that was formed by their Federal Constitution, then the military becomes a force of tyranny. Thus the military no longer becomes the guardian of the people. If they are used for military action without Congress making a declaration of war, this becomes a contradiction in defending our freedom; and Congress can only make a declaration of war on other Nations.

The Constitutions of both Nations of the United States and of the Confederate States need to be updated to allow a special military force that is separate from the regular military branch to be used only when their nations are attacked by terrorism that is not supported by any other nation. But if it is proven that some nation was behind the terrorist attacks, then Congress must declare war.

Lock And Load

Under the Federal government of the Republic, the federal constitution and the State constitution cannot be denied nor be controlled in a way that would violate the rights of the citizens of the member States. Nor can the Federal and State constitutions be transformed in a way that would be a contradiction to that which has been written within a Democracy, it's a whole different story. The right to keep and bear arms is a right that belongs to every citizen that is under the jurisdiction of the states and their Federal Constitutions. Both the constitutions of the Confederate States and the United States have protected this right of the citizens, in that it is we the people who are the voice to speak out, and to vote, including being the militia that defend our constitutional rights. It is also true that it is we who are the very last defense against anyone that invades us, be it a foreign Nation or our own Federal and State governments.

Tyranny has no boundaries when it comes to loyalty to a distinct people. Tyranny has no boundaries when it comes to the loyalty to a Country or Nation. Tyranny only has one loyalty, and that is to oneself. To allow yourself to compromise your rights of self defense and the tools that are needed to enforce that defense, gives your permission for anyone to also decide what rights you may have or if you should have any rights at all. The division between the hunters and those with the civilian assault rifles is a debate that should have never happened. The hunters have no concern about what the law may do to those who have pistols and assault rifles, because they feel that it will not affect them at all. They are very wrong in their way of thinking. In history, it has always been the hunters and the city folks who have fought together in order to defend the sovereignty of their rights. The violations upon the arms of the civilians will have an effect upon the hunters in the near future, because it will be the hunters who will be using the same weapons that belong to the civilians. It will be that time when the war is at our doors and on our States soil.

Another threat to us and to the United State is this: the continual loss of corporations and factories. Not only has this hurt the income of everyone's families, but it also affects the ability to make weapons and so forth against invasions and the ability to resist against more tyranny. When the world government is put in place, the people will not be able to stand against them. You can thank the United State government for that. It was their idea to bring these other third world countries up to being equal as far as the economy goes, so that they would be able to function within this new world order. With our jobs being moved to other countries and our borders not being protected from illegal aliens, North America is becoming a third world continent. I also find it very distasteful to think how these corporations can condemn our birthright and our true identity. Yet they will have their business in communist countries. It's all about what is politically profitable; and they don't mind violating our constitutional rights, especially when it's not politically profitable.

The N.C. Creed's Objectives

The purpose of this document, The North Carolina Creed, is a set of principles for each one of us to live by. Self-preservation is the key to this document. For when we preserve the existence and the rights of our people, without denying the same to others who are not of our own, we have set an example for others to do the same. "Compromising is not an option." Compromising is "destructive within itself". Emotion and the unexpected situations have caused everyone to be hypocrites some time or another.

For an example, as God has put the Ten Commandments upon the tablets of stone, and as our Founding Fathers had also put the words of The Declaration of Independence and The Constitutional Rights upon those papers, so the words that you will find on The North Carolina Creed shall always be a continuous reminder of the duty that falls on us all. So make copies for others, then sign your own copy. And always live and stand by these principles. Persecution is always to be expected, but justification shall be our truthful outcome. Thank you for your time.

JOHN T. NALL
SALISBURY, N.C.
3 JULY, 1997

North Carolina Creed

20 May 1997

As a citizen of The Tar Heel State of North Carolina, I ask all North Carolina citizens, who share the same views as I, to sign this North Carolina Creed.

I refuse to recognize any consolidated government that is not a Constitutional Republic *of North Carolina.*

I also condemn all forms of cultural and racial genocide *toward my people and toward those who are not. I also denounce any* Constitutional Rights *to those who are not legal* citizens within the Confederacy. *Equality in the eyes of man does not violate the proof of the evidence of God and the balance of nature; and only by having a true form of justice that is true and noble can there be* equal justice before the law. *I shall also* refuse *to obey any laws that would violate the* laws of Almighty God. *The laws of* God *and the principles of* our founding and Confederate *forefathers shall always be* supreme in this Southern American state. *I shall defend these truths with all of my* honorable Rebel might*!*

BY: MR. JOHN T. NALL

_____   _____
N.C. CITIZEN SIGNATURE   DATE

The North American Profiles

The North American profiles will be done on the personality of the history of the United State of America and of the Confederate States of America. This subject is not based on the bloodlines of these two Nations. Nor is it that these two Nations are not without sins. This subject is based on their personalities alone.

The United State of America

1. They believe that they are the right hand of God, from the time that they had invaded our Confederate Nation to this very present.
2. They believe in the might makes right theory.
3. Their moral principles are based on their present economy and political views during that present time; and it is always changing.
4. They have always put their faith in technology instead of God.
5. They believe that chivalry is a sign of weakness.
6. They believe that they are above and beyond approach.
7. their treaties and promises are always changing with the seasons.
8. They have made great advancements in technologies.
9. They have come to the aid to other nations that have been invaded by far more extreme tyrannical invaders.
10. They have done wonders in space explorations.

Therefore, the personality of the United State of America should be known as *The Land Of Cain*.

The Confederate States of America

1. They believe that any form of aggression or any form of aggression that requires military resistance.
2. They believe in chivalry because to them it is a sign of self-control and a symbol of a civilized society. And without it, they would become like savages or wild beasts that roam the wilderness.
3. They believe that since they were victims as a Nation at the hands of the United State of America. That the world would have sympathy for their oppression and imprisonment into the Union.
4. They believe that history is their only testimony of their actions and that God shall vindicate them in his own way in his own time.

5. Their love for the Constitution as as equal to their love for the Ten Commandments.
6. They have a habit of bickering among each other and losing their focus on matters that are far more important above their personal views and social status.
7. They have, in the past, been guilty of taking their eyes off of God and giving themselves the recognition that had belonged to the creator.
8. They are quick to humble themselves when they realize that they have done wrong toward their God Almighty.

Therefore the personality of the Confederate States should be known as *The land of Abel*; but slowly the Confederate Nation is being transformed into *The land of Cain*. The majority of Nations fall under the category of the land of Cain; and the minority of the Nations will fall under the category of the land of Abel. But this personality profile can just as easily change over the years. For an example: The Confederate State falls under the profile of Abel, because it is a Christian Nation; but because of the outside influence of the United State, the Confederate Nation is transforming into the land of Cain. The United State falls under the profile of Can because the Christians in the United State are the minority of the population and because the society and government show no presence of Christian influence.

The personality profile can just as easily be used on individuals also. Both profiles are a part of everyone's daily life. Yet one may be stronger than the other. So let's look at the profiles of Cain and his brother Abel. As you know, the story of Cain and Abel comes from the Old Testament book of Genesis.

CAIN

1. He is the symbol of mankind without God
2. He is also the symbol of the world in darkness.
3. He desires to worship God in his own way.
4. He takes pride in the works of his hands and dares to give the fruits of his labor as an offering to God.
5. He cares only for himself and cares not of what he has done to others.
6. He believes that he does not need to answer to anyone.
7. He is the Empires and tyrants of our world history.
8. Therefore he is the dark side of Mankind.

ABEL

1. He kept God in mind first before all things, even in his offerings to the Lord.
2. The Animal fat from the first offspring as a burnt offering from Abel was the symbol of the coming of Christ.
3. He cared enough for his brother to give him counseling, and his brother took his life.
4. His obedience to God is a sign of humbleness and commitment.
5. As a shepherd he understands the meaning of being a servant first and being a leader last.
6. He is not filled with envy and jealousy of others.
7. He is a symbol of man with God.

8. Therefore the dark side does not divide him from his creator.

This is just a quick understanding as to the idea of who Cain and Abel are as individuals, for the Holy Book doesn't give us much information on the subject. But it is enough for us to have some sort of understanding as to the effects of sin and how it can show the effects in the personalities of individuals and Nations. *In the spirit of Abel, we cling to Christ Jesus; but in the flesh of Cain, the world and the sin thereof is tugging at our hearts.*

The United States Of Mexico

A people who are making the struggle each day to provide for themselves. A Nation that is rich with heritage and resources, and yet they struggle in their daily lives just to get by. The Mexican Americans are filled with problems that haven't improved over the years. The Mexicans' problems have become not only a burden to our Confederate Nation, but also to the Nation of the Union. The illegal Aliens who have risked their lives to violate our laws and trust do not do so for the sake of freedom and because they care for our people and our Nations' safety. They are doing these things because they are living below poverty level; and they are desperate to survive as a family. They have no respect for our heritage and our language; and by these actions, they have made a mockery of those who came here to be legal citizens. If we cannot trust them to obey this first simple law, then we are unable to trust them with keeping any other State and Federal laws as well.

The reality is that they are colonizing among us and in our small towns; and this would be an act of war. By all rights, the government of the United State would be in their legal right to make a declaration of war toward the government of Mexico; but they will not do so, for they have been bed partners with the Mexican government just as they have with other Nations as well. The people of the United States of Mexico have, on many occasions, made many revolutions toward their own federal government; and every time that they have overthrown that government, they have put new people in office and yet kept the same form and system of government. Thus the problem continues to repeat itself. The government to the United State has given a tax write off to any business that would hire them as a quota; and these same businesses would hire them, knowing when their papers were not the real thing.

Business and especially small business will hire them as cheap labor and let their higher paid employees go. Slave shops or sweat shops have been found in the big Northern cities of the United State. Not only do these people come here illegally, but also state and federal laws cannot constitutionally protect them. The federal government of Democracy has been using the constitution as a defense of these invaders; however this does not make it constitutionally legal. Strange as it may seem, illegal foreigners have more constitutional rights and protection than the citizens of *Democracy of this United State*. Companies have moved to Mexico for the sake of cheap labor, or slave labor if you will. I make this statement because they will pay them as little as possible and is not a plus boost for the company of that Nation. They will increase more jobs but not with financial improvements and security; and they have done damage to the incomes of the families of North America.

These Spanish people have invaded us illegally and are unable to see and understand how they have taken jobs from our people, jobs that put food on the table and keep the roof over the heads of our children. They understand not that they have offended and insulted us by not learning our culture and language. Nor do they care for the things that are dear to us as a people and Nation. Nor do they understand that we cannot welcome them with open arms since they are uninvited guests that are abusing our hospitality. At time they think we are a funny and strange people because they don't understand the way we look at life and the way we see the relationship of ourselves as a people and as a Nation. They don't take everything to heart the way we do. Nor do they believe that a person should take their problems out on everyone else. At the same time, we are unable to trust them because they have no respect for our laws and for us as a people. I should also say that they are not the only ones who are coming over here illegally. Other Spanish people from other countries are also coming over here illegally as well; and not every Spanish person is an illegal citizen. But the majority of them are. Those who have become citizens, and have gone through the legal process that everyone else has gone through, should be treated with respect at all times.

The Mexican government could put a stop of these violations; however, they do embrace it because it creates extra income for the Mexican Nation. It's the income of the Yankee currency that these Mexicans are sending back to their families in Mexico, plus the extra tourist money that the Mexican Nation is making. Also, this Mexican government believes that a new world order is coming; and they don't want to be left behind. They think that if they join t his World Empire that they will get their peace of the pie. But, in the end, it is they who will end up with egg on their face. The Mexican Americans have, more than once, tried to have honest people run for governmental offices; but they would always be assassinated. Thus the people are always living in fear. I cannot tell these people what is the best form of federal government for them. I can only make a suggestion to them; and that would be for a constitutional form of government. This would mean that they would have to have another form of revolution. I'm not saying that my idea is perfect, because I don't know about their States constitutions, nor am I sure if they even have one.

However, the federal government is keeping all of the wealth while their people live in poverty. The Mexican federal government is also known to violate the human rights of all of their people, yet we never hear anything about it. The United State government is gaining a lot in this game also. While the big businesses is having a big influence on the federal government and thus giving the politicians security in office, the United State government is also working to create a multicultural society that is without having North American cultures, which would cause the North American people to cling too. Finally, the Union federal government needs a new angle for future political gains in the near future. And that, my friends, would be the Race card. The truth is that the Negroes of North American have been used up to the point that they are unable to advance the careers of these politicians. By taking these illegal aliens and making them citizens, this would create another racial block of voters that would be used against the majority. In the end, the black folks will be in the same boat with us white folks.

By rights, the government of the United State should tell the government of Mexico that they must stop all violations of their people from invading North America. They should tell them that human rights must be established for all of their people; that they must submit to the voice and the will of the people of the United States of Mexico; and if they don't, then a declaration of war will be passed in the congress of the United State. The last thing that the Union government can do is to stop all North American tourists from crossing the borders. There should be a heavy prison term, without parole, for anyone that is transporting illegal aliens across the North American borders, including people that make fake documents for any reason. I do have a lot of friends from Mexico and from El Salvador; and I do care for their future. I have worked with them over the years, but I know that most of them have not earned the right to live here among us. Doing that which is right must also come before friendships.

Lost In Space

One of the greatest ideas that brings fear into most of the minds of our people is the thought of other forms of life outside our Earth. The idea of something that might be smarter than us could be a threat to our false illusion of our own greater intelligence. Some people believe that maybe the religions of Mankind come from the visitor from space. It could also be that some Christians may also believe that nothing else could be out there, because it was not mentioned in the Bible and the fact that it could mislead others from Christ. I can truly say that I can understand how they may feel this way; however, I believe that if they were meant to be child of Christ, then nothing of Earth and in Hell could ever stop it from taking place. The Bible is a manual of how we may have relationship with our creator. Even more so, it is the explanation of the relationship between everything that has been created here on Earth and how it affects our daily lives.

At times you may find that the Bible doesn't have all the answers to all of our questions; and you may find it to be kind of odd that it doesn't. Basically the Bible was written based on a *NEED TO KNOW BASIS*. The whole world could not hold all of the information, if it was written into the Bible. Nor would the extra information help anyone to be saved from the sin and the decay of this world. The Bible only covers the basic highlights that we need to know: where we are going and the salvation to save Mankind. Unlike the opinions of some knowledge in itself is not a salvation nor is it power to overcome all things. Knowledge is a tool; and we are limited as to how we may use it for the betterment of Mankind. But one thing is clear to me, and that God is the one who creates all things, whether it is from the past to our present and into the future. And into this day, he is somewhere and everywhere, creating his creation; and being a God that he is, He will also establish some form of life that will be connected to it in some way.

How logical would it be to think that God would create other universes and not establish some form of life therein? I am not saying that God is creating other forms of life in his own image. Nor am I saying that he is giving other life forms a living spirit. But it would be a false belief on our part to think that God had stopped being a creator after he made Mankind.

God has given Mankind the desire to explore and to learn about the things that are around us,, and that which we are made of. It just could be that the Christians may someday, in spirit, journey into the unknown where our physical selves cannot go.

So if there were other life forms that have visited our world, what do they want with us? Most likely they are explorers just as we have explorers of our own. It is very possible that some people have suffered from the experiments that have been done to them, basically the same that we have done to animals here on Earth. It could be that they may still be learning about life just as we are still learning ourselves.

However, I do not believe that they are coming here to take over our world; and I can give you two reasons why. The first reason is that our God would not allow it, for the simple fact that the fate of Mankind has been sealed within the scriptures of Revelations. The second reason is the fact that Mankind would be more dangerous to other life forms from space than they would be to us. The reason that Man is more dangerous is because of the fact of the sin of the flesh. Greed, fear, and hate, including selfishness, would be the key factor that would endanger other life in space. Another thing we need to remember is this: God created us to function within the cycle of life here on Earth. It would be self-destructive for us to drift too far from our home planet. Clearly we should remember this one and important thing: that we have done very poorly in taking care of our own planet; and until we complete our responsibility in doing so, the last thing we should be doing is establishing colonies on other planets. In truth, Mankind is not ready to explore too far into space. Mankind must complete their own journey of self-exploring before they are ready to stretch too far out into the stars. One of the greatest tragedies is that a few people have reached out to welcome the beings from space to come and to greet us in peace, while all the time Mankind is not ready to welcome them. So in the fate of the aliens who do come would be the death of them. Another strange thought has also come to my mind. It just could be that since we have been made in the image of our creator, these beings might believe that we may be the key to their existence.

Sometimes we do get too big for our britches; and we become overeager to rush into things when we are not truly ready for it. It hasn't been too long since we as children of this universe just began to learn how to crawl. We are not capable of running, let alone walking just yet. It's time that we slow down some and make sure that our progress here on Earth is running at the same pace as we are reaching out to the stars. Progress takes time and patience as well as perfection. We should learn to balance the three of them while we are moving forward into the future.

Other Truths

The ideology of liberty is transformed into principles that are brought forth into words and is brought to life upon the pages that shall define the understanding of that liberty which had been paid for in blood. It cannot be written in a way that would remove the principles of its meaning, nor should anything be written in a way that would counteract it and cause that portion of that liberty to become null and void. For as it is true that all forms of words have meanings, therefore it also defines the meanings and the intentions by those people who stand behind those words. Anything that is pure in honesty to the liberties of our people can quickly be transformed into bondage by others with evil hearts. Freedom is never regulated and privileges are never free. Freedom can never be found in ignorance or in being gullible. We must come to know those words that define our freedom or the freedom that our people once had. We must come to respect and to understand it and most of all to guard it with our lives. For the liberties that had been established for us were not intended to remain only as an opinion between our ears. No, my dear comrades, it comes with actions and responsibilities that we are held accountable for. And if we are not held accountable and we start to compare our freedom to the rest of the world, then indeed, we have lost our way!

By: John T. Nall
10-July-03

Understanding Freedom

As each day that passes by us. We are filled more with the confusion of the meaning of freedom. The very understanding of this word brings conflicts among ourselves. And the reason for this is the ideas of past freedom are not the same of the present ideas of freedom today. Freedom comes in many forms and can cause conflicts to the definition of its meaning. The definition of freedom for a nation is defined also differently from the others as well. For it is something that is clear cut and without gray areas. It is straight to the point and does not come into conflict within itself. It is the principles of ideas that give other nations the free will to embrace. it can not be forced upon others. And it can not transform into some other form that would be a contradiction to its foundation. It can not be given freely without the cost of blood. For to do so is to deny the future generations the ability to understand the meaning and the value of its purpose.

It comes with responsibilities and obligations to preserve and maintain the foundation that sustains all of the other liberties that are founded upon it. It has no comparing to other ideas of freedom and oppression that are founded by the ideas of those of other nations. It has only its own reflection to look upon. And is unable to see any other reflection than its own. It does not violate the rights and the justice to those that are protected by it. And like all other forms of beauty, it can be stolen and trampled upon by those with evil hearts. And her name is ***A CONSTITUTIONAL GOVERNMENT OF THE REPUBLIC***. She is the closest idea of liberty that our God has given mankind, within this physical realm. For not only does she follow the principles of God's holy word, but she is able to hear the voice of the people. And though she is not spiritual liberty that is guaranteed through Jesus Christ! She is, however, a blue print of what an earthly government should guide itself by.

John T. Nall

League Loves South

Certain media reporters have given false information to the public as to what the *League of the South* is all about. Ignorance plays some part in this; however, the majority of it is bigotry toward the Southland and her people. As president of the *Zebulon B. Vance Chapter* of the *league of the South* here in our beloved city of Salisbury, I should clear up a few things. We welcome all Southerners who love the old Confederacy and her people and believe in Christian values to join this great and noble organization, regardless of race, age, sex, or even if you're born in the North. We believe in the real form of government, which is the republic, and we have no desire for North America – and especially the old States of the Confederacy – to become a third world country.

Therefore, we do not support the socialist programs of diversity training or those who persist in compromising our Southern birthright. Our identity and our heritage, as well as our values, are no longer for sale. Gen. Robert E. Lee finally came to realize that it is far better to die a free man than to live under the heel of tyranny. This was when he had regrets about surrendering at Gettysburg. God save the South! – John T. Nall

---

25 of May in 2001 – of the Salisbury Post Newspaper in North Carolina

The World Trade Center Prayer

On behalf of the *Confederate people*, whom you have always known as *Southerners*, our hearts go out to the people who have died, suffered, and may still be alive at this time underneath the destruction of the towers. It brings sadness upon us all whenever destruction falls upon any people for any reason at any time. *We pray to You, our Heavenly Father, that you will have mercy upon those who have died during the time of this tragedy and the collapsing of those towers. We pray and ask of Thee, Dear Lord, that You will reach out to those who may still be alive. Moreover, that You will bring them out from the rubble and return them safely to their loved ones. We also ask the same for those who have died by the same actions within the Pentagon in Virginia. Also for those of the airline that was under the same situation in Pittsburgh, Pennsylvania. We ask, Dear Lord, that You will comfort the families of those who have lost someone, and that You will help them to be able to pick up the pieces of their lives and start over once more. Have mercy on them all. In Jesus' Name*

Amen.

15 of September 2001
By: John Thomas Nall

We are asking every true Confederate to pray this prayer and to fly all flags of the Confederate States and state flags at half mast, for seven days.
Thank You and God Save The South!

This statement was put on the internet as of this day forward.

A Letter Of Recommendations

I, John Thomas Nall, am making a list of recommendations to the future Congress of the Confederate States of America. After our federal government has been reestablished, during a peaceful and non-military action toward the United State of America, request that the representatives of the people from the member States of the Confederacy take my person request under consideration and make amendments to our National Constitution of our Confederate States of America. Thank you, and may God bless our Confederacy.

1. Request that *A DECLARATION OF SOUTHERN INDEPENDENCE*, written by John P. George, Jr. of Crawfordville, Georgia CSA, be drafted as the official Declaration of Independence of The Confederate States of America; and until that time that is done. Let it then be the unofficial document of our occupied Confederacy.
2. That the States establish border patrols between the said states of the Confederacy and the states of Mexico and of the United State. The other member states that are not on the borderline of other Nations are to work as equal members with the member states that are on the borderline with these Nations. That the federal Government shall not use its power to patrol these borders, but instead patrol the Inner coastal ways of the Confederacy and use the Confederate Navy and Air Force for this standard mission.
3. To override and eliminate all constitutional rights to own and to sale of human slaves, regardless of race, age, sex and gender.
4. To establish a free trade with other Nations, as both federal Constitutions of North America would recognize the United State being equal partners in this trade act.
5. Establish a treaty with the United State and England, and with Scotland and Ireland, providing they are no longer part of the English Empires (Britain). A treaty that the Confederate states will make a declaration of war toward any Nation that would directly invade the Nations of this treaty and that the Nations of this treaty will do the same also.
6. To forbid any funding to the member states to be used for public or Government schools.
7. To make it unconstitutional for the federal government to establish public or federal schools within the member states of the Confederacy.
8. To forbid the sale of land to any corporations that were not established within these Confederate States.

9. To only allow all foreign corporations to lease property within the Confederacy, providing that it is within the standards of the laws of that said State.
10. To deny any foreigners the right to live, work, or own any business within the borders of these Confederate States, until they have become legal citizens.
11. To deny any State and federal constitutional rights to any persons that are not legal citizens of the member states of this Confederacy.
12. To deny citizens the visa rights to go to any countries that might be presently hostile toward the Confederate States.
13. To use all means necessary to defend the citizens of these member States against a hostage situation and against terrorist situations without violations of the protection of the citizens' State and federal constitutional rights.
14. To classify it as unconstitutional to use forced integration and segregation upon the citizens of these member states, that all public areas are for all citizens.
15. To recognize that freedom of associations is a constitution right.
16. To only make war toward the terrorist group that has directly been responsible for the attacks toward the military and civilians of the Confederacy.
17. To establish a *Prime Directive* Guide Line for all military and representatives of the government of the Confederate States of America of non-interference with the cultural and present form of government, including the technology of any Nations with whom they come into contact, and to establish a strong disciplinary action toward any one that violates this directive.
18. To revoke or to denounce any citizenship to any persons of birth and of non-birth for making or copying information or any federal or state government forms and photographs for any reasons without being the government of the Confederate States or of the States government. And to have that person or persons removed forever from these States of the Confederacy. Examples: passports, visas, birth certificates, deeds, licenses, etc.
19. To establish a permanent Air Force.
20. To establish a permanent Special forces group of Air Force, Navy, and Marines for search and resuce and for emergency situations at non-war times.
21. To clarify the definitions as to the rights of the States and of the authority of the federal government and President of these Confederate States of America, during the times of war and of foreign invasions.
22. To establish *The Salute to Our Southern Cross* for our final official National Flag, as is written within this book.
23. To establish the extra taxations upon property after it has been paid for to be illegal and unconstitutional.
24. To deny citizenship to a person born within the borders of these Confederate States, providing that child's parents are not citizens of this Confederacy.
25. To denounce a *dual citizenship* as unconstitutional and disloyal.
26. To deny citizenship of thirty years to anyone that violates our Confederate borders illegally.
27. To permanently deny citizenship to anyone having a criminal records from other Nations.

28. To permanently deny citizenship to any aliens guilty of smuggling any form of substance and materials across our borders for not going through the proper customs.
29. To recognize that Christianity of the gospel is also the foundation of our federal government and that Christianity will not be forced on others, but will be protected by federal law.
30. To establish the *22 of February* as a National Independence Holiday, with holiday pay.
31. To denounce the draft as unconstitutional, except in times of invasion of our Confederacy by another foreign military force.
32. To recognize that the people of these Confederate States who are in sound mind and have no criminal record to be the militia or home guard, as a last resort of home defense and fall under the jurisdiction of the state governments. And to clarify in what way it shall stand in relation to the military of the federal government.
33. To recognize that the State citizen of the majority and of the minority has the same rights under their State and federal constitutions.
34. To recognize it as being unconstitutional to use the state and the federal government as a tool or to impose military will on the citizens in social engineering.
35. To forbid anyone to hold any office of the State and federal governments who has held any office within the Empire of the Union, in order to protect the citizens from the corruptions of the ideology of centralism.
36. To denounce any form of *Affirmative action* including *Apartheid*
37. as acts of discrimination and unconstitutional.
38. Requesting that our former President: Jefferson Davis' birthday be a National President's Holiday.
39. To establish a National Memorial paid holiday.
40. To establish a system wherein a citizen can serve in the National military and is later, if willing, able to transfer to one of the States military service and still be able to keep the same rank and pay.
41. To allow women to serve in the home guard or the States Military, but to deny our Confederate women from being in harm's way when they are serving in the National military.
42. To reinstate the Dragoons as the Special Forces as or with the marines. Jefferson Davis created the Dragoons.
43. To prevent any more blockades of our coast ways in the near future.
44. To recognize Agricultural slavery and Industrial slavery, including sweat shops, as falling under the institution of slavery and to protect the citizen workers from falling into these situations.
45. To establish *OSHA* programs for the safety of the citizen workers.
46. Classify lobbying in Congress as unconstitutional and illegal.
47. To establish a strong law against politicians being bought.
48. To deny the federal and State governments from asking information and using the income or the race of a person, including their gender, for any reason at any time.
49. To establish a space program for the military defense of our Nation and our border Nations' neighbors. And for the basic use for our society.
50. To establish a permanent savings account for every Confederate citizen instead of social security, insuring that from ten to twenty percent of that person's income will go into their savings

account. And that they are unable to withdraw it until they have retired from the working class. Plus the interest that they receive from the bank.
51. To work with the States governments, with work programs and so forth, in helping the street people get back on their feet once more.

A Day Of Fasting And Prayer

I, Jefferson Davis, President of the Confederate States of America, do issue this my proclamation, setting apart Friday, the 27thday of March, as a day of fasting, humiliation, and prayer; and I do invite the people of the said states to repair on that day to their places of worship and to join in prayer to Almighty God, that He will preciously restore to our beloved country the blessing of peace and security. In faith whereof I have hereunto set my hand at the city of Richmond, on the twenty-seventh day of February, in the year of our Lord one thousand eight hundred and sixty-three.

Dear Compatriots:

The 27th of March is a legal holiday within our beloved Confederacy however un-active because of the present foreign power that is at hand. However! This can't prevent the state governments of the Confederacy from making it a state holiday with a day off of work and with pay. So I am asking all state governments to pass a bill that would make this a legal paid holiday and stated for the reasons that were made by our beloved President Jefferson Davis. Thank you and God Save The South!

John Thomas Nall

Despised by the World

They can deny it. They will truly condemn it! Even when "It" trembles the ground beneath their feet. For your enemies will truly stand against it! To purify it by fire, then with baptism of water, it is still as transparent and pure within itself. The clock of time cannot lay its grasp upon it, so it never shows wear with the ages of time.

    Mankind has spilled an enormous amount of blood to protect that honor. Others try to destroy it out of fear and hatred. It shall be heard and will not be denied; and a price will always be paid. That drifter of life. That lonesome warrior who only deals with the facts. It's name is the "undeniable truth".

14 MAY 1997

"Government Control"

The best way for a government to keep society under its control is to keep its people ignorant of their political rights and of their history, by lack of knowledge and the use of half truths.

Let us not drink from the cup of our enemies, for their drink may be filled with deception. Nor should we lay down our arms and put our bodies and the bodies of our children into slavery just for the name of peace.

21 FEBRUARY 1995

Southern Chivalry

I set my principles high above my emotions and physical desires. I am responsible for all of my actions, knowing that they may affect the outcome of my people and country. My relationship with my God and my family shall always fall upon the things that I do and the things that I do not. I shall always stand for the truth and true justice in all things. The principles of my founding and Confederate fore father did not die in vain, for they continue to live through my daily life. I was born into this world with nothing except the family name I was given. As I leave this world with nothing, I shall protect that honor that falls upon my family name. I was created by God and Southern by birth, and I will strive to always keep my word. The war between my mind and heart and desire shall not always be at peace; but I must protect these principles that stand for the things I care for. Doing what is right may not always bring me joy and happiness, but I will become less without it. I am by how I live my life, by the principles that make me more than what I was before.

John T. Nall 2 May 1998

Knights Of The Golden Circle

To the Copperheads of times past.

Thank you for your support in defense of the rights of my Confederate Nation.

You have established the first resistance in the defense, for your Union of the Republic.

True patriots, in defense of our founding forefathers.

For you had clung to the truth of liberty and struggle to save your Nation's rights.

Traitors toward tyranny, you stood against the majority.

In choosing right over might.

You have made a place of honor in our hearts and minds.

And you have become mortars of constitutional liberty.

On behalf of our Confederate people.

                                                                      Thank you

A Salute To Our Southern Cross

I salute the Flag of the Confederate States of America,

In memory of the gallant men, women and children

Who lived, loved, suffered and died

Fighting for the right to be free

Under God,

With affection, reverence, and undying devotion

To the cause for which it stands.

AUTHOR AND TIME WRITTEN UNKNOWN

We, The People

As time slowly passes, the future is sure to come. Generations of them, who have been lost, will come to know who and what they are; and their Southern Cause shall be a lost cause no more. Truth is the justice that's within, of itself, for it stretches from the heavens and down upon the four corners of the earth. They shall embrace one another as a people once more; and as they hold their Third National Flag up high above them, they will give praise and thanks to their God for their country. Their voices will spread throughout their land, the voices of singing their song of "God Save The South".

29 APRIL, 1998

"The Battle Cry"

As we left our loved ones to the side, we have now not known as time goes by to give our blood to The Tree of Liberty and then come to embrace our Master's Cross. Never to question our purpose and cause, we march into battle with our Flag of Saint Andrew's Cross, never forgetting that our blood and tears have watered our land. To save our liberty, we took that stand. Never worry as you may pass our grave sites, for we're in Christ's hands now. He'll not pass us by! We sacrifice our bodies for those whom we love, for our country to stay free from the tyrants' tide of that union, who shall forever try to rule our country with an iron glove. We have done our duty and paid that price; and we know not what has become of our country and people as time passes by.

And as you think of us, remember us true. Fill your hearts not with sorrow, but only with pride. As your tears begin to flow, remember why we died. *"Fear God, men; and you'll have nothing else to fear."* Let these words flow from your heart to your tears.

John T. Nall
19 July 1999
Salisbury, N.C. C.S.A.

Babylon The Great

Oh! Babylon,
    The great Yankeenites.
What has become of you?
    For you have become astray.
Rejection of your Nation Founders.
    And the imprisonment of your cousins Nation, of the Confederacy. Treason of your rejection in your minds toward our Founding Fathers.
    Treason of your hearts toward the Father of all creation of things.
Tell me the truth,
    Can you not see the blindness and the madness that has overtaken you?
Does not the stench of death come from your Nation's Banner?
    Tick for tack and kill for that.
For lies and power and control of this and that.
    You've become overwhelmed from the numbness of playing your Russian roulette.
The taste and smell of "treason" is upon your tongue and in your nostrils.
    Death and decay have become your Nation's foundation.
Bones of your conquests and interferences in other nations.
    Determining to control the minds and hearts of the people of the world.
Your self Delusions of Grandeur have overcome you,
    and the world has become the Objective to be transformed into your vision of life.
Where is it written that the crown of "world power" should be placed upon your head?
    Lay your head to rest and think on these things.
Neither Nation nor Country should rule over another.
    Not even in the name of liberty or peace.
It is not the place of Mankind, but only for our Majesty, King Jesus.

To Remember Me By

To remember is not enough

To honor is to only remember

But to be thankful is to act upon that gift

And to act upon that gift is to make it a part of our daily lives

In honor of our Confederate People

Who fought in preserving of our State and National Independence

Thank you! For all that y'all have done for our Nation and Country

On behalf of our people and of our Families

Lest we forget

Deo Vindice

A Dedication To Our Confederate People

Cast your sorrows and tears into the depth of our graves
    Let your hopes and dreams be comforted by the heart of our Lord Christ
In truthfulness of righteousness
    We must strive in walking that extra mile in reaching toward the light
        of His glory and of love of our God
    To deny the catastrophe of this world, from binding us in our faith in Christ
Soldiers of the King of light, is triumphant over the soldiers of the prince of darkness
    In this spiritual and physical war, in Him we shall lean upon
A Christian Nation, we must strive to live as one
    Against all invading Nations and of spirits of damnation
And by His own will and understanding
    And in His own way, God will vindicate

A Southern Toast

To our Christ and Confederacy The devotion of our cause Constitutional liberty, and a sinless life that is our daily strife Three cheers for all that which we hold so very dear to our hearts.
Hurrah!   Hurrah!   Hurrah!

John T. Nall

Statements Of Truth

❧ "I am with the South in life or in death, in victory or in defeat... I believe the North is about to wage a brutal and unholy war on a people who have done them no wrong, in violation of the Constitution and the fundamental principles of government."

-- Major General Patrick Cleburne

❧ "All that the South has ever desired was the Union as established by our forefathers should be preserved and that the government as originally organized should be administered in purity and truth."

-- General Robert E. Lee

❧ "We feel that our cause is just and holy; we protest solemnly in the face of mankind that we desire peace at any sacrifice save that of honour and independence; we ask no conquest, no aggrandizement, no concession of any kind from the States with which we were lately Confederated; all we ask is to be let alone; that those who never held power over us shall not now attempt our subjugation by arms."

-- Our First President: Jefferson Davis, 29 April 1861

❧ "If we were wrong in our contest, then the Declaration of Independence of 1776 was a grave mistake and the revolution to which it led was a crime. If Washington was a patriot, Lee cannot have been a rebel."

-- General Wade Hampton, CSA

❧ "The principle for which we contend is bound to reassert itself though it may be at another time and in another form."

-- Our First President: Jefferson Davis

❧ "People separated from their history are easily persuaded."

-- Karl Marx

❧ "We could have pursued no other course without dishonour. And as sad as the results have been, if it had to be done over again, we should be compelled to act in precisely the same manner."

-- General Robert E. Lee, CSA

❧ "The history of an oppressed people lies hidden in the lies and the agreed-upon myth of its conquerors."

-- Meridel Le Sueure

Y"None are more hopelessly enslaved than those who falsely believe they are free."
-- Johann W. Von Goethe

Y"The right to be let alone is indeed the beginning of all freedom."
-- Supreme Court Justice William Orville Douglas

Y"The only thing necessary for the triumph of evil is for good men to do nothing."
-- Edmund Burke

Y"I gave my loyal and enthusiastic adherence to the present, with all its fresh and glorious possibilities; but I shall never forget that it is to the Old South that the New South owes all that is best and noblest in its being."
-- Thomas Nelson Page, 1892

Y"The Confederate battle flag represents all Southern and even Northern Confederates regardless of race or religion and is the symbol of less government, less taxes, and the right of people to govern themselves. It is flown in memory and honor of our Confederate Ancestors and veterans who willingly shed their blood for **SOUTHERN INDEPENDENCE**."
-- Dixie Outfitters

Y"Let us be certain that our children know that the War Between the States was not a contest for the preservation of slavery, as some would have them to believe. But that men who fought were warriors tries and true, who bore the flags of a Nation's trust, and fell in a cause, though lost, still just, and died for me and you."
-- J. Taylor Ellyson

Y"Thy name shall be a name of proud. Thy heroes all have nobly died. That thou mayest be the spotless bride of liberty, my Dixie! Then wave thy sword and banner high, and louder raise the battle cry. Till shouts of victory reach the sky, and thou art free, my Dixie!
-- General Robert E. Lee

Y"Stand Southrons! Fight and conquer, solemn and strong and sure! The fight shall not be longer than God shall bid endure. By the life that but yesterday waked with the infant's breath! By the feet, which are, morning may tread to the soldiers death! By the blood which cries to haven crimson upon the sod! Stand, Southrons! Fight and conquer. In the name of the mighty God."
-- Unknown

Y"We have fought mighty battles, and our deeds of valor will live among the richest spoils of times ample page.'
-- First President of our Confederate States: Jefferson Davis

❦"I can only say that I am nothing but a poor sinner, trusting in Christ alone for salvation."
-- Confederate States General, Robert Edward Lee

❦"The human male is able to take a difficult situation and make it simple, then later turn around and cause a simple situation to become very complicated.
-- John T. Nall

❦"Surrender means that the history of this heroic struggle will be written by the enemy, that our youth will be trained by Northern school teachers; learn from Northern school books their version of the war; and be taught to regard our gallant dead as traitors and our maimed veterans as fit subjects of derision."
-- Confederate States General Patrick Cleburne

"Nothing is more certainly written in the book of fate than that these people are to be free. Nor is it less certain that the two races, equally free, cannot live in the same government."
-- Thomas Jefferson

❦"The great rule of conduct for us, in regard to foreign nations is in extending our commercial relations to them with as little political connection as possible ..."
-- First President of the USA, George Washington, in his Farewell Address

❦"After the South had been conquered by war and humiliated and impoverished by peace, there appeared still to remain something which made the south different – something intangible, incomprehensible, in the realm of the spirit. That too must be invaded and destroyed; so there commenced a second war of conquest, the conquest of the Southern mind, calculated to remake every Southern opinion, to impose the Northern way of life and thought upon the South, write "error" across the pages of Southern history which were out of keeping with the Northern legend, rising and unborn generations upon stools of everlasting repentance."
-- Frank Lawrence Owsley

❦"If the South had been an Independent nation for the past 30 years   it would have had budgets more closely in balance, less governmental taxation, a tougher policy on crime and welfare, greater local control over schools, protected prayer in schools, a more conservative Supreme Court, and an immigration policy that would not flood the country with Third Word immigrants."
-- William L. Cawthon, Jr.

❦"The Gettysburg speech was at once the shortest and the most famous creation in American history. The highest emotion reduced to a few poetical phrases. Lincoln himself never even remotely approached it. It is genuinely stupendous. But let us not forget that it is poetry, not logic; beauty, not sense. Think of the argument in it. Put it into the cold words of everyday. The doctrine is simply this: that the Union soldiers who died at Gettysburg sacrificed their lives to the cause of self-determination. That government of the people, by the people, for the people, should not perish from the earth. It is difficult to imagine anything more untrue. The Union soldiers in battle actually fought against self-determination, it was the Confederates who fought for the right of their people to govern themselves."

-- H.L. Menchem

▼"The Civil War wasn't just a victory of North over South. It was a victory for a centralized government over the States and federalism. It destroyed the ability of the States to protect themselves against the destruction of their reserved powers. Must we all be happy about this? Abraham Lincoln himself, the real Lincoln that is, would have deprecated the unintended results of the war. Though he sometimes resorted to dictatorial methods, he never meant to create a totalitarian State. It's tragic that slavery was intertwined with a good cause, and it is scandalous that those who defend that cause today should be smeared as partisans of slavery. But the verdict of history must not be left to the simple-minded and the demagogic."

-- Joseph Sobran

▼"I feel that you are free men, I am a free man, and we can do as we please. I came here as a friend and whenever I can serve any of you I will do so. Therefore let us stand together. Although we differ in color, we should not differ in sentiment."

-- CSA Lt. General: N.B. Forrest in Memphis, Tennessee, July 1875.

▼(War Crimes) 600 Confedcrate American POWs were marched from Ft. Delaware on 20 August 1864 and were placed as "Human Shields" in the line of fire at Morris Island, S.C., to protect Union troops from Confederate Artillery. They faced starvation, exposure, disease, and the incoming fire of Confederate Troops for a total of 45 days.

▼"They that can give up essential freedom to obtain a little temporary safety deserve neither Liberty nor Safety."

-- Benjamin Franklin

▼"On 18 June 1865, Edmond Ruffin, a preeminent Southern Nationalist "fire-eater", who had been one of the leading antebellum proponents of Southern secession, chose to commit suicide rather than submit to the subjugation of Yankee bayonet rule. Defiant to the bitter end, this fiery Southern patriot penned these famous last words in his diary just minutes before taking leave of the Yankee tyranny that had descended upon Dixie: "I here declare my unmitigated hatred to Yankee rule – to all political, social and business connection with Yankees and to the Yankee race. Would that I could impress these sentiments, in their full force, on every living Southerner and bequeath them to every one yet to be born! May such sentiments be held universally in the outrage and down-trodden South. Though in silence and stillness, until the now far-distant day shall arrive for just retribution for Yankee usurpation, oppression and atrocious outrages, and for deliverance and vengeance for the now ruined subjugated and enslaved Southern states! . . . And now with my latest writing and utterance, and with what will be near my latest breath, I here repeat and would willingly proclaim my unmitigated hatred to Yankee rule – to all political, social and business connections with Yankees, and to the perfidious, malignant and vile Yankee race."

-- Edmund Ruffin

❧The battle flag does not belong on the graves of our Confederate dead, not unless you expect the dead to rise again in the defense of our Confederate Nation. The Confederate battle flag belongs to the past, present, and future military forces of the Confederate States of America and must only be flown during a Declaration of War. Nor does it belong to the non-enlisted. Give the honor that truly belongs to our defenders of liberty that are now lying asleep in their final rest and let their Nation's National flag (The Third National) be flown forever above them. Let not our dead heroes' graves be desecrated by the Union National Banner, for this has been known to have happened in the past.

-- John T. Nall

❧"The Southerners should be treated as a conquered alien enemy."

-- Thaddeus Stevense

❧"Sir: We congratulate the American people upon your re-election by a large majority."

-- Karl Marx, letter to Abraham Lincoln, congratulating him on re-election as President of the United States, January 28, 1865

❧"There was no surrender at Appomattox and no withdrawal from the field which committed our people and their children to a heritage of shame and dishonor. No cowardice on any battlefield could be as base and shameful as the silent acquiescence in the scheme which was teaching the children in our homes and schools that the commercial value of slavery was the cause of the war, that prisoners of war held in the South were starved and treated with a barbarous inhumanity, that Jefferson Davis and Robert E. Lee were traitors to their country and false to their oaths, that the young men who left everything to resist invasion and climbed the slopes of Gettysburg and died willingly on a hundred fields were rebels against a righteous government."

-- The Rev. James Power Smith, last surviving member of Jackson's staff, 1907

❧"I'm an honorary black member of the sons of Confederate Veterans and there are probably hundreds of camps across the south with folks whose ancestors fought for the Confederacy and earned a place of dignity and I know that black folks also earned a place of honor under that flag."

-- H.K. Edgerton

❧"All the people of the South struggled through the war and the Jim Crow laws and segregation, that was forced upon us under the stripes. It was the stars and stripes whose representatives brought slavery into America. And not under the Christian Cross of St. Andrew, that represented Jesus Christ. The Cross of St. Andrew is just as American as the Betsey Ross flag or the Star Spangled Banner."

-- H.K. Edgerton

❧"While it has been proven that the Confederate States of America is and has been a separate Nation in every way, yet ideology-wise the Confederate States of America does not temporally exist at this moment. The mental reconstruction or transformation of the minds and hearts of our *Confederate American people* has caused us to reject the concept and philosophy of our Founding and Confederate Forefathers. We have been conditioned to care not and to reject our own culture. We believe that this Southern culture is something of the past that was evil and that it has no definition as to who we are now. After all! We believe that we are *Americans* and nothing else. Therefore this culture cleaning against our Confederate people and our occupied Nation goes without restraints from outsiders. Our Confederate American people, regardless of the differences of race, are no longer standing together as a people of a particular nation. Therefore our people have become like chattel without concern for others except ourselves. This is what we must overcome. For it is not enough to have a Birthright, we must embrace it and relearn that part of our true selves that we have been conditioned to reject: that is who we are and what we are and what we were meant to stand for as *Confederate Americans*. Until then, we shall not be free."

-- John T. Nall

❧"We may not always approve of the actions of the *United State government*. Nor do we, as Confederate Americans, condone any actions of violence of any kind that is not of self-defense."

-- John T. Nall

❧"All I can say is that there's a sweetness here, a Southern sweetness, that makes sweet music. If I had to tell somebody who had never been to the South, who had never heard of soul music, what it was, I'd just have to tell him that it's music from the heart, from the pulse, from the innermost feeling. That's my soul; that's how I sing. And that's the South."

-- Al Green

❧"Racism used to mean in inherent hatred and contempt for certain races, a belief that certain races were fundamentally evil and unworthy of existence. Now the word applies not only to those who are afflicted with neo-pagan race hatred, but also to those that have any shred of loyalty to their own inheritance, their own culture, kin, and community."

-- Robert Salyer

❧**WAR CRIMES.** This was Sherman's attitude toward Southerners during the war of Southern Independence as well. In a July 31, 1862 letter to his wife (from his Collected Works) he wrote that his purpose in the war was: "Extermination, not of soldiers alone, that is the least part of the trouble, but the *Southern People*". His charming and nurturing wife Ellen wrote back that her fondest wish was for a war of *extermination* and that all *Southerners* would be driven like the Swine into the sea.

Book title is **THE REAL LINCOLN** BY Thomas Dilorenzo.

❧"There is a certain class of race problem-solvers who don't want the patient to get well, because as long as the disease holds out they have not only an easy means of making a living, but also an easy medium through which to make themselves prominent before the public."

-- Booker T. Washington

❧"I have fought against the people of the North because I believed they were seeking to wrest from the South its dearest rights, but I have never seen a day when I did not pray for them."

-- CSA General Robert E. Lee

"Knowing that intercessory prayer is our mightiest weapon and supreme call of Christians today, I pleadingly urge our people everywhere to pray. Let there be prayer at sun-up, at noonday, at sundown, at midnight, all through the day. Let us all pray for our children, our youth, our aged, our pastors, our homes. Let us pray for our churches. Let us pray for ourselves, that we may not lose the word, for those who have never known Jesus Christ and redeeming love, for moral forces everywhere, for our national leaders. Let prayer be our passion. Let prayer be our practice."

-- CSA General Robert E. Lee

☨Dear Heavenly Father: Be with thy people in our hour of trials. Grant those who misunderstand and malign us the integrity to find the truth and honor it. Guide our heads and hands to your Holy purpose. We pray in they Son's Holy name and for His sake. Amen

-- (*Dedicated to our Confederate Americans of past, present, and future*)

☨I have a deep respect toward the memory of *The United States of America* and of her Declaration of Independence and of her National Constitution. I have a deep respect for the constitutions of her member States. But I have no love for the new America that is known as *The United State of America*. I have no love for their Democracy and of their foreign occupation of our Confederate Nation of member States. I have no love for their false truth and for that which it is to represent, for it is the majority of my people that do not know nor dare to accept the real truth. Nor can I say that based on the ideology of our Founding and Confederate Forefathers that we are truly free.

-- John T. Nall

☨William Z. Foster, had of the Communist Party in the 1940s, stated in his book *Toward a Soviet America*: that the American Soviet will, of course, abolish all restrictions upon racial intermarriage . . . that the revolution will only hasten this process of integration, already proceeding throughout the world with increasing tempo.

☨"As a Nation that was established by our Founding forefathers, of a Constitutional Republic of Sovereign States, "States Rights" is no more. Only in the Title and the Symbol of a bygone Nation, thus remains of the United States of America."

-- John T. Nall

☨"The children of the Devil are just like their father, because they are both liars."

-- Kenneth Hagin

☨A Constitutional Compromising is when anything is added or is taken away that would cause a particular right to become null or void or that would break the principles of that constitution on the foundation that it had been founded on. The perfect example would be *The United States Constitution*.

-- John T. Nall

Have You Ever Longed For . . . . .

Have you ever longed for that perfect love? Have you ever had the desire to love someone with all of your heart? And never having the fear of that someone rejecting your love? I know that I also do. Have you ever wanted to find someone to understand you and to be your friend? A love that never grows old or never lets you down. So many times people will be looking for that special someone. That perfect love, from a man or a woman. They will spend most of their lives searching for something that no average human being can give them. But that love is as close to you as your lips and the tip of your tongue. And you can only find that love within the words that you would speak. As you bring those words to life, your actions will show that those words that come from your mouth are not lies. But they are words that are coming from your heart. Your true self is stepping out to unlock the door that shall open up to the meaning of the value of your life. That special someone is Jesus Christ. God the Father, who loves you so much that He had His Son to die in your place in order that He may have the relationship with you that He was not able to have with you before. Death, which is the sin that has stood between you and Him, is no longer a wall that stands in your way. He will not walk away from you nor shall He ever withhold His love from you. He has sent His Son, on His behalf, to offer His love to you. To reject His Son's love is to reject His own love, because one cannot understand the true meaning of love and not become a member of the family. That is what He wants from you, to join His family. Are you looking for that perfect love? Then here is what you need to do. Repeat this prayer out loud.

My Heavenly Father: I ask that the blood your your Son shall wash away my sins, because I know that I am a sinner. I thank you for sending your Son to die in my place and for giving Him victory and raising Him up from the grave. I accept Jesus Christ, who is your Son, to be my Savior; and I ask that You will give me the baptism of the Holy Ghost. I also ask that You will give me the wisdom and understanding and guidance. Use me in your own way to do your will in everything within my life. I love You, Lord. In Jesus name, Amen.

The next step is to find a church that He wants you to take part in and to receive the baptism of water. This will be a Testimony to everyone of Christ washing away your sins and the new person you have become. I pray that our God will bless and protect you and your loved ones.

John Thomas Nall

Compare this building to America's foundation today,
and see how we have deteriorated.

By: J.T. NALL
December 17, 1996

Confederate National Crest

The Confederate National Crest is a dedication to all of the Confederate Americans
of the past, present, and of the future, regardless of race, creed or gender.
It is a reminder to our people of the fact that we are to always be a Christian Nation
and of the fact that we are Confederate Americans.
The words *Deo Volente* are Latin for *If God Is Willing*;
and Psalm 91 is a scripture that every Christian Confederate
American should come to embrace in their heart
The Confederate National Crest is not the creation of the
Confederate States' government or of its member states
May we always be humble and put the will of God first, trusting in Him to protect us.
Amen
By: John Thomas Nall
(This caption was placed below the picture in the original.)

Continuous Balance

In order to better improve my personal life,
I must follow the path of my "Lord Jesus Christ".
For He is my guidance and teacher of life.

And through Him,
I'll be able to do what is best for my family,
my people, as well as my country.

As a continuous cycle, that has not an end,
where all things in life that are separated and yet connected,
can only be the true balance in our lives.

Dedicated to: James Terran Knight and Amber Nicole Knight

By: John T. Nall
23 January 1997
Salisbury, N.C.

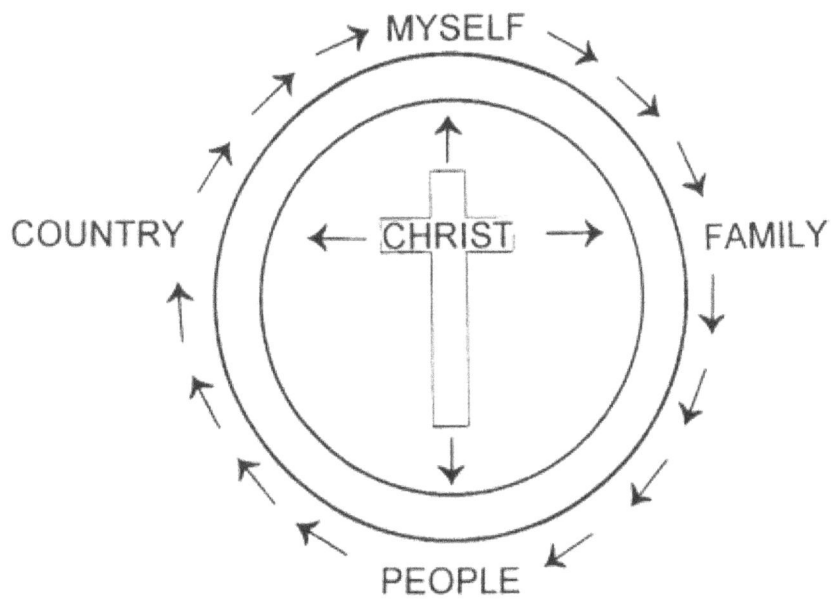

The Glory Of Jehova

Our Father:

    We take a step back in remembrance of the glory that we did not give you before. We forget at times that when the odds were against us, it was Your glory and not our abilities that won the battles for our country. Just as it was You Who have spared our people to continue on. Yet when we forgot our place, You stepped away from us. We lost our freedom to the union foe. Without You, Dear Lord, we cannot stand on our own.

    To always put You first and to give You Praise and Glory and Thanks is the very first thing that we as a country should learn and always remember. So, forgive us when we forget our place, Dear Lord, for now and always. Let not our Confederate people fall short from Your understanding, for it is far better to fear that You would depart from us as a people and as a nation than to fear those who trample upon our liberties that were given by You. As long as we put You first, then it shall also be You Who will be involved in everything that we do. Praise be Jehova's Name!

By John Nall
13 December 1999
Salisbury, N.C. C.S.A.

In All Glory And Honor

I am the voice and my son is my hand.
    With love and care, life was brought before us from within the nothingness;
And everything else was made to sustain all life.
    Look at my testimony,
For my creation is the evidence of my Glory.
    Look upon my own likeness and the many verities thereof,
For he is known as *Man*.
    Look at the verities of all other forms of life
And dare not to deny my right of recognition.
    Look at the testimony of my love to you,
For he was sent to you as *Christ*.
    He is the reflection of my love as he is my hand,
For how could I share my love to you without reaching out to you?
    Take heart!
For a blind man can see more of things than those who can see,
    For those with vision put trust in their sight alone.
But in your spirit and sight, The evidence is clear.
    Therefore you know who I am and you know my son.
And to know about me is not as becoming to knowing me through my son.

In Your Presence

Oh Lord, let me stand in your shadow.
    Oh Lord, let me stand in your light.
Oh Lord, let me stand before your presence.
    Oh Lord, let me walk by your side.

Oh Lord, let me stand beneath your shelter.
Oh Lord, let me be drenched by your grace.
    Oh Lord, help me to always remember
That at your table, you've saved me a place.

                    Amen

Thanksgiving

It is a day of celebration,
a day to give thanks,
and to give or share our time with our family and friends.
A celebration of home cooking and desserts.
It is a time to remember and to forgive everyone concerning all things.
It is a day to remember the meaning of true friendship
between two different kinds of people,
just like the friendship between the
Native American Indians and the Christian pilgrims.
It is a day to give thanks and praise to the Lord for all things,
to give time to give thanks to Him for being with us during
the good times and the ones that were bad.
It is a time to remember the times when Christ was not in our lives,
and of how we have grown from within since that time.
It is a time to show our love.
And it is a time of remembrance.

My Hero!

For Christ Jesus is The Declaration of my Independence.

That goes far beyond my physical self.

HE is the Key that has unlocked my heart

    and released my self from the bondage of sin and eternal death.

HE is the Gateway as I am the traveler who passes through.

HE is the Lighthouse, and I am the vessel that was once lost on the stormy seas.

HIS light shines upon me and guides me safely to shore.

HE has laid His footsteps upon His Father's righteous path,

    so that I can place my feet upon His footprints.

I am transparent, through Him,

    for He is my King and I am a soldier in His service.

He is my Vindicator, as I have pledged my devotion to Him.

I give all that I am to Him, for He is the One and Only True Mentor.

John T. Nall
20 February 1999
Salisbury, N.C. C.S.A.

"Oh Lord"

Oh, Lord, let your glory shine through me.

Let me, in the end, become your perfect masterpiece of your work.

Let your will become mine.

As I ask that my eyes shall always be upon you,

Let my love for you be seen within my life.

From day to each and every day, let your peace dwell within my spirit,

And your words upon my lips.

Let your love remind me of my self worth, so that I can carry my cross,

Just as your Son has done for me;

And though people may reject my love.

Yet it is always you who are knocking at my door.

I ask that I dwell not upon the things that I cannot change,

Or upon the things that I do not understand.

But only to always trust in your words during my time of sorrow and pain.

For I have chosen to be that which you want in me,

In Your Precious Name.

John T. Nall
3 January 2000
Salisbury, N.C. C.S.A.

Soldiers of His Majesty

The world is your battleground, where the forces of darkness are waging war against the forces of light. But this war has been won in advance! Yet it's the battles within this presence. So stand tall, soldiers of Christ! For the world look upon you as being the true knights of shining armor. It is your breastplate of righteousness, which guards your heart. Your helmet of salvation, that you wear, is a symbol to those who stand against you as well as to those who shall accept your King in time to come. That belt of wisdom that's around your waist is a reminder of your Creator Who has opened your eyes.

So hold your shield of faith up high! As you trust in your King and your King's Father, you are not alone and you are not on your own. Because you have been marked by the Holy Ghost, it is He Who is greater within you than he who is in this world. This means you have been chosen; and forget not yet the sword of the spirit which hangs by your side. For the Word of God does not yield; and He knows not the meaning of the word "compromise". From time to time, you will need to regroup, for those soldiers who will stand on your left, with the others on your right, are your one and only brothers and sisters of Christ.

Humble yourself always in the presence of the Lord, as it is that wherever you go, He is with you. When you're asleep or awake, He is near. And as your last breath slips away, He is waiting for you. For what value does a warrior have without a King? And being a warrior that you are, which would be harder: To die for your King or to live for Him? In the presence of His majesty, it's all the same.

So listen once more when I say to you: Stand firm in the gospel, as it will bring you peace. And fear not, as your King went forward before His army and has won this war in advance. The shadow warriors and their prince of darkness are a constant memory of defeated foes. So be ready for Him. Soon you shall see the return of your majesty.

30 MARCH 2000

True Love

Oh Lord! How great is your love?

You have touched me in a place where no one else can reach.

You whisper to my spirit, with your deep and gentle embrace.

You took me into Your family and gave me peace.

You sent Your Son to die in my place.

Your words have become the water that quenches my thirst,

Just as Your words feed the hunger within my spirit.

It is Your stream of promises that run through the fields of my life.

To love You with all that I am is how I am able to love everyone else.

Your love, given to me, has enabled me to learn to love myself.

By casting my cares at the feet of Your Son's cross,

I am able to make it through another day.

And what more could I ever come to ask of you, my Lord,

except to someday hear You say: "My child, it is with you that I am well-pleased".

22 JANUARY 2000

Bendito Sea Jehovah Para Siempre

Oh Lord, You and Your Son are so precious in my sight! I think not of the gifts that You've stored in heaven for me, for what is greater? The gift or the One Who has given the gift to me? And how could the gift come to have any meaning to me if it is not given to me out of love? But yet it is You, my Lord, Who is my Treasure! For you have given Yourself out of love to me. As your salvation is the ticket that has paid my way into heaven, forever within Your Presence. And so, how could I compare any other gifts to this? So let my love be forever Yours.

As there is truth in Your words, where the Holy Spirit brings Your words to life, it is Your Holy commands that open my eyes and enables me to see, so that I may know whereupon I may put my feet in walking in Your path of righteousness. Just as it is my enemies who are blind and strike at everything that is near, just as it was destined to be. Praise be the Lord forever.

Hear Our Voice

He came to us, where life begins,
in the birth of innocence, in purity,
as He is the Lamb.

So let this world fall in silence,
as upon that moment the heavens shall hear them say,
"No King but Jesus; for He has come".

He gave to us what we did not know, what was lost.
To those before and after Him,
who are His flock.

So let this world fall in silence,
as upon this moment the heavens shall hear them say,
"No King but Jesus! For He has come".

For loyal and faithful is He
to bring forth His Father's plans:
to reach out to all who are in need.
Like water, He cleansed all those who received Him.

So let this world fall in silence,
as upon that moment the heavens shall hear them say,
"No King but Jesus! For we wait for Him to return!"

The glory of His Father, which filled the heavens,
so shall then come to renew this earth.
Just as the Son of the Father took the first
step in establishing our salvation,
in His natural birth.

Are You Ready?

PEOPLE GET READY!

JESUS IS COMING!

HE'LL BE COMING SOON!

CHILDREN GET READY,

FOR CHRIST IS COMING;

AND HE'LL BE TAKING US HOME SOON!

ASLEEP OR AWAKE,

IN THE NIGHT OR AT DAY,

LET US GIVE THANKS,

FOR HE IS ON HIS WAY!

NOT BY OUR TIME,

BUT BY HIS,

SO LET US ALWAYS PRAY.

SHOUT TO THE WORLD AND SHARE THE GOOD NEWS

AND SAY:

PEOPLE GET READY!

THE TIME IS COMING SOON!

22 September 2001

Trinity Of God

1. Your love is like the waves of the ocean, which overwhelms my body.
2. Your Light that shines from you is more than my eyes can accept, yet you bring no harm to my sight.
3. Your presence overcomes my fragile body, which magnifies all of my senses so that I am unable to move by my own free will.
4. Yet to be consumed by you once more is the same desire as an infant who never wants to leave the mother's womb.
5. As you are the beginning and the end, so then it is also that you are the center of the universe, for all of your creation is all around you.
6. It was through the Holy Blood of your precious Son that I was purified. By dying in my place, he became my mentor.
7. It is your words that live within me, as I give my spirit to your Holy Ghost, who is now my counselor.
8. It is you who desires our love, just as it is your Holy Book that shows us how to give our devotion and our love to you.
9. To kneel before you in prayer and to glorify you with every word upon my lips.
10. To be transparent as others see your glory through me.
11. To pick up my cross and follow my majesty.
12. And to lay these words of yours upon this paper; and to thank you with every breath.
13. Yet nothing that I do or say could ever give the praise to glorify your name.
14. So let me worship you forever from this life to the next.
15. And let my brothers and sisters in Christ be the sample of your glorified name.
16. All glory be to the Trinity of our Lord God Jehova! Forever and ever Amen!

John T. Nall
10 November 1999
Salisbury, N.C. C..S.A.

My Love

Where can I go? Moreover, where can I hide? Except to be safe in your arms, to hold you dear so very near within my heart.

The value of my life that was paid in full, that perfect love that I could not find, that no one else could give, except that I long for it deep within my soul.

At times, I feel lost and alone. However, I know that my feelings are not always true, for I trust in your promise,, oh Lord. Moreover I stand on your word.

In addition, I know that you are always near. You are my hope and dreams, and you are the love of my life. The tears of joy that have watered my face, as it is the blood of Christ who had died in my place.

Let me not forget the value of my worth as you teach me the ways of your love, that love that never fades, nor never becomes lost in the passages of time.

Death for death and life for life!

    For was it not your blood that has covered mine?

        Was it not your love that has paid my price?

Yes!

    And I thank and love you Lord.

From: Tommy Nall, 3 of June 2001
I dedicate this poem to my friend: Jamie Peeler
Lexington NC CSA

Lonesome Dove

Your beauty is filled with the gentleness of your heart.
Such sweetness, as of honey.
And in the hour as the moon is of high.
To hold you close, by my side.

Your love I shall embrace.
Your passion I shall caress.
Let nothing stand between us.
As our love intertwines into one.

To love each other in Christ.
Our love becomes secured.
Such a lovely fate between us.
That others shall come to adore.

Oh! Let me not be forever apart from you Miriam.
Let me not be lost as a dove.
For in my heart is a place of emptiness
That could only be filled by your love.

Oh! So sweet as wine and that never bitters with age.
I can only hope in time, for your love to embrace.
I long for your presence and companionship.
To hear your gentle voice.
To touch you and to caress you.
I long for your love.

Dedicated to: Miriam Beatriz Tobar Hernandez
By: John Thomas Nall
2 of July 2004

Twinkle Stars Afar

They twinkle down seemingly oblivious
To the pain in my heart,
Or do they just see something that solves the equation?
Or someone that lives beyond the horizon?
The first one said, "My love has died".
The second one said" I feel I should cry".
And the third one said, "It's not worth the try".
After each goodbye I glare through the tears
Of the stars which are smeared and ask why?
The spirit will guide me up past the pains as
turtle doves glide after the rain.
The divine celestial crown comforts me.
For they see all the forest and not the trees.

By: Terri Nall / 1995

In Honoring My Parents

I can think of the times of my younger days and of how I longed for that bonding between a son and his dad. It helps me to realize the importance of love that a child needs from time to time, that constant struggle to set the ideas of manhood in me to follow. You became a role model at the time of my birth; and the lessons that you have taught me have become the golden rule in my relationship with others. I look not at you in the perfection of manhood, but as a dad who has done his best to love and teach his children as best he could, and to do so as you struggle to learn the meaning of fatherhood. Indeed, it is a great honor to hold your baby in your arms and to tell the world that *this is my son* or that *this is my daughter* and to have the title of FATHER.

So many times you have come to my defense. You've shown your gentleness with a sign of firmness as to the error of my ways. You have sacrificed so much for the ideology and the meaning of *a family*. You are the peacemaker in this family of ours and a diplomat to all of the creditors all around. At work and in the home your job is never done. From sun up till the time that it goes down your job is never done. Dealing with each day you take it as it comes, in hope that someday your family will remember your love: the love of a MOTHER.

That spark of love between a Man and a Woman, as the two become one and complete, then begin a new journey as new members of life join the family. The struggle to help the other in the times of growing and learning of one another including of ourselves. To care and teach and to protect the other. To provide as we grow as a family. We struggle to correct the errors of our children, in hope that it will not follow them for the rest of their days. To hope and to dream that our children will have the fulfilling of the dreams that we may not have had. The greatest joy that a parent can have is to see the joy and the dreams come true in the eyes of their child.

A DEDICATION TO MY PARENTS

My Closing Statement

I would like to thank you for taking the time to read this book project of mine. I also hope that you were open-minded enough to give my words some thought. I would like to make it clear for everyone that my views and philosophy are based on my understanding of history and the observation of the changing of the times. These views are not necessarily the views of the proofreader who has worked on this project, nor are they the views of any organizations of which I have a member. My way of thinking may not always be perfect, and yet I am never too far from the truth. The common sense and wisdom that I do have are a reminder to me to give thanks to my creator for all things. I am not doubtful that my views will be offensive to someone. That is just a part of life; and those who are offended should learn to live with it. People are always doing something to offend me, including you, as well. I would like to give thanks to everyone on Earth and in Heaven for bringing this dream to life. Thank you all; and may our Christ Jesus dwell within all of you. Y'all take care.

John Thomas Nall

www.ingramcontent.com/pod-product-compliance
Lightning Source LLC
Chambersburg PA
CBHW081345070526
44578CB00005B/726